It's Not My Mountain Anymore

By Barbara Taylor Woodall

To Carolyn

I hope you enjoy

Barbara Woodall

Catch the Spirit of Appalachia, Inc.
WESTERN NORTH CAROLINA

FIRST EDITION 2011

Layout: Amy Ammons Garza
Cover: The Woodall's grandson, Sterling

PUBLISHER
Catch the Spirit of Appalachia, Inc.
Imprint of Ammons Communications
SAN NO. 8 5 1 – 0 8 8 1
29 Regal Avenue • Sylva, North Carolina 28779
Phone/fax: (828) 631-4587

Library of Congress Control Number: 2011930760

ISBN: 978-0-9827611-9-9

ACKNOWLEDGEMENTS

I am deeply grateful to God for placing these precious friends in my path. Friends are gifts that come from HIM. Each one helped me bring *"It's Not My Mountain Anymore"* to fruition:

To long-time friend and fellow Foxfire staff member Laurie Brunson Altieri who has supported me from the first word to the last. Our excellent rapport made this book possible. Laurie put her life in Virginia on hold and brought her editing expertise to the North Georgia Mountains in tireless efforts;

To Pat Rogers, Margie Bennett and Eliot Wigginton, all former Foxfire staff members and mentors who offered superb guidance;

To Ann Moore, current Foxfire President—a kinder soul with her phenomenal patience would be hard to find;

To Bob Justus a local poet for continual inspiration;

To Virginia Watts, Rhonda Conrad, Jason Airlie, Dr. Bob Wells, Ruth West, Chevin Woodruff, Dorothy Ann King, Connie Moore and Martha Darnell, extraordinary friends who contributed their thoughts and encouraged me in weary seasons;

To Catch the Spirit of Appalachia for help in publishing;

Last, but never least, to my family who lost me to pen and paper far too long;

I am indebted to you forever.

For our children Melissa and Isaac
And
Their children's children
And
For our Appalachian heritage

CONTENTS

CONTENTS

Description	Page

Part III
"It's Not My Mountain Anymore"

Mountain Solace

INTRODUCTION

"The range of the mountains is his pasture, and he searcheth after every green thing..." Job 39:8

A pasture is a feeding place that sprouts green morsels of nourishment for hungry creatures and provides rest in green shady groves near rippling waters. My pasture is the portion of the beautiful Appalachian Mountains located in North Georgia.

According to the Wikipedia Encyclopedia, scientists believe our mountains are the fourth oldest chain on earth. They are millions of years old, birthing more kinds of life than any other. Ancient glaciers from the north dropped thousands of seeds, producing vast vegetations including plants used for medicine.

Old timers say the name "Appalachian" means "People of the Other Side" and derived from the Apalachee Indians living here before Spaniards arrived. The secret of the mountains in all their majestic power and calm uniqueness lives within Appalachian people who abide in green pastures.

There is a fascination here that holds rich and poor, strong and weak captive, not with chains and fetters but by an almost touchable solace that affords many visitors an escape from city rat races.

Any disclosure about the Appalachian

Mountains captures national attention. ABC network's award winning documentary, "Hidden America: Children of the Mountains," captivated over ten million viewers because in large part, my people are hidden to America. We are in fact, "People of the Other Side." We remain separated from urban America by endless mountains, unique folklore, damnable stereotypes and fierce independence.

Our famous and beloved <u>Foxfire Magazine</u> and over a dozen books have been an important recorder of our mountain culture, preserving the memories of a way of life that is a living part of our collective American heritage. The books have sold over nine million copies. I was supremely blessed to have been a part of Foxfire's early years. I want to share with you the inspiration that it gave to my bored and straying teenage mind and the lasting impact it has had on my life.

I wrote *"It's Not My Mountain Anymore"* to share with you a vanished lifestyle that I once knew and loved as a child reared in a humble mountain home within a loving farm family. The mountain I once knew is not the same. Inevitable changes both to the landscape and its inhabitants clash harshly with cherished memories of a passing era I long to recover.

Beautiful mountain scenes are now disrupted by elite housing, streetlights, increased traffic and paved roads. The great mountain ridge that overlooks what was once my close-knit family community on Kelly's Creek is now a high-dollar development. Across the road and in plain view are eight rental trailers housing strangers speaking strange dialects. Nights are no longer reserved as a time for peace and rest. Continual traffic breaks the still of the night with loud mufflers and blasting radios. We don't know our neighbors anymore.

Dad once said, "The time will come when you'll have t' lock your barn at night."

That time has come.

Mountain Hospitality needs no formal invitation, so drag up a chair, cock up your feet and feel free to help yourself to a tall, ice-cold glass of sweet tea as I share mountain experiences and the many colorful people that have shaped my life. Taste the harsh realities of change. It's a journey filled with appreciation, humor, love and loss. Take what you want and spit out the bones.

PART I

PLANTED NEAR THE WATER

*"The Lines are fallen unto me in pleasant places;
yea, I have a goodly heritage..."* Psalms 16:6

I was born into a mountain heritage to Jim and Cleo McConnell Taylor, February 4, 1954. Mama was born to Irish parents, Edna Ledford and Bill McConnell, October 24, 1918, in nearby Macon County, North Carolina. She was one of eleven children destined to work family lands for survival.

Grandpa McConnell was crippled with arthritis, depending on crutches to walk. The disease wrapped around his small frame like tightening vines around forest trees. Someone told Grandma McConnell to dig earthworms, boil them and make poultices, but the endless efforts to ease his pain failed.

His disability prevented him from doing physical labor aside from driving mules pulling loaded farm wagons. He reined in farm animals and eleven younguns using a bull whip with a beeswax cracker. A cracker is tiny shreds of leather on the end of a whip. Beeswax kept it supple, and it made loud sounds like gunfire when quickly jerked in the air. The cracker served as a warning to heed commands when ploughing. Mama said, "One time I cut drive with a rock at sister Pearl. Blood gushed down her face stinging

13

her eyes. I thought I'd killed her. When Dad returned with the wagon and heard what happened, he said, "All right, Cleo step up here. He popped me three times with that whip. I could have run away into the fields, but we all respected him. I had wonderful parents."

My McConnell relatives spoke with strong Irish accents. We wanted to search their pockets for green shamrocks and funny leprechauns. Mama shared many memories of her early childhood.

"Grandma Edna made wine for medicine which she kept in churns hidden deep inside the root cellar wall. Brother Ralph had a taste for it. His nipping caused him to paint a mule blue. That caused quite a conversation in the community. Another time, Ralph filled the well with tin cans just for meanness." Mama remembered walking ten miles to the store to get lamp oil carrying a small metal jug. Just before she reached the store, she removed the small screw-type lid on purpose because the storekeeper would plug the filled jug with a slice of orange candy. Once out of sight, she popped the candy in her mouth and replaced the lid.

Mama was eighteen years old when she caught the Tallulah Falls Railroad to Georgia to visit Aunt Inus. That's how she met and later married Dad on April Fools Day, 1937. They jested that they both got fooled.

My parents hatched half a dozen children in their quiver. There are twenty-years between my oldest brother and youngest sister.

Mama said it was like having two families. The first three- Edward, Betty, and Ellis- were yoked to work. Work is a four-letter word; so are food and love. Edward and Betty worked alongside Mama, as baby Ellis played on a padded quilt spread in the corner of the corn patch. Mama put syrup on his hands and gave him a feather. It was a wonderful, simple pacifier uncomplicated by batteries and cords. My older siblings had all but flown the coop by the time Ernest, Beatrice and I came along. My parents must have been tuckered out "raisin" younguns. They just named the last three in their quiver and turned us loose.

Laughing Irish eyes made it hard to tell when Mama was really mad. They looked like clear pools of blue water where fairies danced and pipers played. We thought she had eyes in the back of her head, hidden by short dark curly hair. Without ever losing focus from inside chores, she knew exactly what we were up to. Nothing escaped her sharp attention. Rebukes filtered from the house like, "All right, younguns; I am gonna help ye out with that scrabble," or, "Get away from that copperhead-infested wood pile! If one bites ya, it will die," or, "Y'all been in the garden trompin' in th' beans; guess you'll eat snowballs this winter." Probably my favorite warning was, "I am gonna whip y'all till ye pee like a polecat, then whip ye for peeing."

She never took a switch to me. I can't say the same about Bea, my younger sister who once slipped down the road without permission. Mama slipped after her with a peach tree switch, dosing her all the way back home. Then she rubbed lotion on Bea's striped legs lamenting over hurting her. Dad said, "It don't do any good to whip, then pet her." Ernest, our slightly older brother, got many thrashings and no lotion.

Dad was quiet, tall and lanky, dressed in baggy, bibbed overalls and work boots. Sawdust settled between the leather laces and on his sweat-stained hat. The dusty hues contrasted with jet-black hair and chinquapin eyes that darted about with sharp glances. His smooth, shaven face was tanned, but roughened by mountain elements. His long-term commitment of love and responsibility fueled muscle and sweat to feed, clothe and shelter the family. His diploma was calloused hands.

It seemed when Dad was not pulling "the money stick" at Ritter's Saw Mill, he lived behind a mule-drawn plough. Before the sun began its journey over darkened peaks to shine right royally on all dominions, he was rattling harness and trace chains at the barn.

The barn was a mainstay on mountain homesteads, housing more than tools and feed. A multitude of memories rests on notched logs and old gray boards. One rainy day my brother and I climbed the wall ladder looking for hen nests, but a fodder fight was more tempting in the barn loft. Fodder was winter feed for our animals. After Dad discovered the damage, he went to the creek bank to break a red alder switch to lay lash.

Another time, we used his huge black umbrella as a parachute. Needless to say, we broke it and crashed into soft hay bales. Mama was always in the shadows during correction times. I could hear her say, "All right Jim, that's enough. Th' next lick will be mine."

Below the barn loft was a gear room consisting of harnesses and trace chains, buckles, cinches and eyes, bridles and bits. It was also a place to doctor sick or hurt animals and a refuge to doze while fresh rain drummed a rusty tin roof. I think God smells like fresh rain.

Afternoons and weekends until dark, Dad was at the barn, or his hands were wrapped in plough lines, guiding harnessed mules through unbroken fields. Resounding plough commands of "GEE" (turn left) and "HAW" (turn right) echoed about the home place as he turned new ground into straight rows behind him.

Dad never saw mere dirt, but envisioned planted seeds and tender plants kissed by morning dew. Faith in a full harvest kept him stepping. I ain't no preacher, but the Apostle Paul said, "Faith is the substance of things hoped for, the evidence of things not seen." Dad saw bushels of shelled corn drying in hampers for seed and bread. He saw winter feed stored among ribbons of cobwebs, hanging through barn cracks and well fed stock roaming the fields. Dad believed faith without work is dead. He often said, "The Lord provides, but He will find me hoeing around the stalk of corn as I pray for help."

Each new row looked like the earth opening its mouth to produce life. Soft silver winds brought scents of pennyroyal and mint from the creek bank, awakening the sap within him. When he stopped for a dipper of cool water, he often picked dandelion blooms that dotted the landscape like golden jewels of Eden. They looked nice on Mama's table.

On winter mornings from underneath thick layers of patchwork quilts, I studied ice crystal formations on frosted windowpanes. Oxygen-rich air burned our noses until Dad kindled a fire in the mud-daubed fireplace he had built from creek rock and red clay.

Long before the rooster's crow, he raked gray ashes with an iron poking-stick, looking for glowing embers. He reached into the wood box for the rich pine splinters and cones to place on the live coals. Gently, he fanned with a paper until bursts of yellow flames appeared. Aromas of pine filled the house. Finally, a leather string latch was lifted, opening a weathered plank door. Dad carried larger sticks from the porch to cross over the young fire. A huge back stick was placed behind the flames. It held heat all day while he was away working at the sawmill.

The morning fire, now ablaze in the fireplace, turned into a rib-roaster. Mama called it a "turn and burn" heating system. Stepping into my brothers' bedroom with a voice of authority, Dad said, "Hit th' floor. More people die in bed than anywhere else. Shake a leg!" An unheeded call was met with a bucket of cold water thrown into their snoozing midst. It always worked.

He assigned chores for after school. Dad was not to be trifled with; nothing short of a hospital stay excused us. He honored the law requiring school attendance, but school was secondary to working the land. My brothers had one foot in the classroom, the other on fallow ground.

As daylight was breaking, Mama finished cooking up a full breakfast— salty smokehouse ham cut the night before sizzled in heavy grease atop the "Red Mountain J" cook stove. After removing it to a bowl, she stirred a cup of strong black coffee into the hot grease. Red-eyed gravy with soft biscuits was a mountain delicacy. Her breakfast call, "Grab it and growl," meant come to the table NOW, otherwise the dog was most happy. I never ate the grease, but preferred buttered biscuits and oatmeal. Each Sunday morning we were treated with chocolate gravy. If anybody asked, "What's for breakfast", she often jested, "Poke and grits. Poke your feet under the table and grit your teeth." She could make a tasty meal out of just about anything. Our family gathered around a plank eating table in assigned places. I sat on a bench between Ernest and Bea to discourage their constant scuffles. He looked for opportunity to aggravate Bea. He would yank her curls or kick at her purse. He called her silly names and made funny faces at her. She'd retaliate by pouring her teeth to him until they both got a whipping. Scuffles were delayed while Dad bowed his head. Simple words of thanks ascended from his heart like the white steam arising from boiling kettles on the wood cook stove.

Once, mealtime was interrupted by frightful meowing and scratching sounds coming from near the cook stove. Ernest had crammed the cat into the kindling box and closed the lid. Mama arose from the table to investigate the mournful sound. She lifted the lid to meet a mad tomcat in the face.

Somewhat startled she looked squarely at Ernest, "You don't know a thing about that, do you?"

He didn't get a "whippin" for that but she did tell us a tall tale: "One time a rabbit stopped by here on his way to "rabbit town" to buy a pair of red rabbit breeches to hide his long tail. I was stirring a big pan of cream gravy with a fork on the stove when it hopped through the rabbit hole in the door. It near scared me t' death. As it hopped back out the door I dashed its tail with hot white gravy. Its long tail melted and turned white. That's why rabbits have short stubs and that's how rabbits got their white tail. It ain't good to skeer people."

Our table held plenty of simple farm foods. Dad said, "Don't eat nothing you wasn't raised on; you will get sick. You don't know what you are eating away from home." He spoke a mouthful of truth!

Processed food labels are like reading Greek. Many products contain more preservatives than food. Our bodies are well preserved. I doubt our dead bodies need to be embalmed. Meats are laced with hormones to hasten production and commercial feeds with antibiotics. If we sneeze in a supermarket line, three people behind us are cured of infection. What have we done? We feel deprived without junk food. Have McDonald's "Happy Meals" ever made us happy? I crave junk food and glow in the dark. I fear spraying my hair; the window might blow clean out of the bathroom. Thankfully, organic farm goods are returning but at a hefty price. We are slowly returning to yesteryear's goodness.

Mountain people have long used natural food

preservatives. Vinegar inhibits bacterial growth and is used to pickle corn, beans, squash, cabbage and other vegetables. Sugar preserves apples, peaches and pears. Salt preserves and cures meats. Last fall I processed 48 cans of vegetable beef soup adding nothing but salt. Soup sure beats a snowball when winter's breath runs us inside for nourishment. It sticks to your ribs and, true to Dad's words, we know what we eat.

After breakfast, Dad reached high above the fireplace for a dry twist of tobacco he had grown in the field, dried in the barn and twisted in single pieces like hairpins. It lay on the fireboard (mantel) high out of reach from us.

Once Ernest sneaked a piece and rolled himself a big-fat smoke. A few puffs brought him from behind the barn white as a sheet and puking his guts out. Dad called tobacco, "a grown man's candy" and his "nerve medicine." Dunking the twist into a whistling kettle to soften the texture, he shoved it into his pocket, picked up a well-packed dinner bucket and left for work at the sawmill.

In the evenings, he shared news and stories from work. Some of the sawmill workers talked among themselves about a co-worker and his nasty wife. She did not keep house; the house kept her. They wondered how in the world poor Sam stood living with her. According to talk, she could "gag a maggot on a gut wagon." Sam said, "Ah, you can get used to anything." During lunch break, the men found a shade and took off their hats, cooling sweat-soaked heads. When they went to the spring to refill water jugs, Sam went into action. He found some dog soap (poop) to smear on each hat brim. Back at work the men complained of an awful smell. As the day wore on, the complaining stopped. At quitting time, Sam told them what he had done, proving his words, "Ah, you can get used to anything."

Each morning after Dad left for work, Mama pulled on black galoshes she called "poop stompers" en route to the log barn. Shuffling her feet over pegged floorboards in the kitchen, she reached for the metal bucket hanging over the sink. Mama said, "If that cow had a motor in her rear end, you could not keep your daddy away from the barn."

We could hear Ole Heif, our fawn-colored Jersey, bawling impatiently with a heavy bag of morning milk.

Milking time was also feeding time for all the family fowl. Speckled guineas flew and floated though the air like drifting leaves, lighting softly in the barnyard. They were dandy watchers, quick to alert us to any invaders or strange activities. They also warned of approaching rain by endless loud pot-racking sounds before it came. Tom, the turkey, displayed a riot of beautiful plumage, strutting like royal majesty, unadmired by silly hens.

Mama entered the feed room to pour generous portions of crushed corn and cottonseed meal into a short hewn log through a hole cut in the stable wall. Enough feed was important to pacify the cow until the chore was finished. She then took her place on "the udder side of life". Four plump teats had to be washed with water carried in the milk bucket from the spring. If Mama didn't get kicked by Ole Heif, she was sure to get a whipping from a cocklebur-infested tail. My job was to hold the tail out of the way. The phrase, "Hold the tail out of the way" became a figure of speech depicting small jobs. I was not allowed inside the stable until Heif's mood was determined.

Sometimes the cow ventured into the briar patch scratching the "milk factory." Tight squeezing of tender teats was more than enough aggravation to set off a rebellious cow. Milking had to be done for two reasons: The family depended on daily milk and milk products plus a cow will go bad left un-milked. Her bag could burst or she could go dry, or worse, get infection.

I would hear commotions inside, then Mama yelling, "SAW! SAWWW!" That is cow talk to calm the situation. It would only get worse, and Ole Heif would begin to kick and spin around, pinning Mama into a corner. Dad always de-horned all the cows for this reason. (They looked funny walking the pasture for days with white diapers around their heads to prevent infection.)

Size did not matter in a ruckus with Mama. She would fight a saber saw. "If you judged victory by size, this cow could catch a rabbit." The scuffle continued. Soon a shiny, dented milk bucket come flying out the door, followed by the cow wearing a boot imprint on her butt.

Usually, Mama returned with a full bucket twice a day if the cow behaved. White foam threatened to run over the sides, as she strained raw milk into gallon jugs. After it cooled, thick heavy cream rose to the top. She poured it into a butter churn that was set aside in a warm place until the milk clabbered. When the contents turned loose from the side of the churn, or the wooden dasher stood on top of the milk, it was ready to churn butter. The lengthy process of churning needed diversions, so in rhythm with up and down motions of the dasher, she repeated:

> *"Come butter come*
> *Johnny standing at th' gate*
> *Waiting for a butter cake*
> *Come butter come."*

Soft, yellow nuggets formed and floated on top of the milk. She used the dasher to twirl and gather the butter compacting it for easy removal. Mama washed the butter in cold water several times, salted, and molded it in wooden printers. Once the butter conformed to the mold she turned it out on plates. The yellow gold had a pretty carved olive leaf imprint. If pressed for time the butter was turned out without printed designs. She joined her thumb with two fingers making tracks like cat paws on the top. Then she'd act surprised, "Lookie there— th' cat stepped in the butter." Buttermilk was poured into wide mouth gallon jugs. At night we poured the whey off the top to thicken the milk. It made white mustaches on our mouths and smiles in our hearts.

I recall Mama going to the store to buy a new churn, only to be directed to an antique shop. The only one available was cracked, with a price tag of $150. Mama said, "Lord, do have mercy! Imagine what a new one could cost."

Milking was always a chore she disliked. One especially unpleasant morning an exasperated Mama said, "I wish that Baptist preacher owned this cow; he'd beat the hell out of her. I do declare and pray th' Lord that I never lay eyes on her again."

She didn't.

Mama made her usual evening trip to the barn with the metal bucket swinging on her arm. Repeated cow calls of "sookjerz!" yielded no sign of Heif coming to the barn. (Sook is a traditional Scotch-Irish cow call and "jerz" was short for Jersey)

All but a stewing Mama searched the pasture for days looking and listening for the clapper in Heif's bell. Bells were important communicating devices. Mama even put them on toddler shoes to know our whereabouts.

Dad searched the pasture for broken fence poles and tracks leading towards the apple orchard. He was convinced Heif had been "cow jacked" since a good cow was a big part of mountain livelihood. Granny Lou shared white blessings from her cow, Patsy for about a week.

Early one morning the sky held black buzzards circling the north pasture like undertakers at the hospital; Ole Heif had fallen into a ditch and broke her neck.

Dad went to get our neighbor, Glenn Hopper, and his tractor to pull the carcass out. A rope was secured, the tractor running. The body was all swollen up like at calving time. The air stunk like carrion; blowflies buzzed around. The dog and I watched from a great distance. As the carcass rolled down the ditch line, air began to escape from its lungs with dreadful sounds. The dog spiked its ears and started howling; my hair stood on end. I wondered if Ole Heif had risen from the dead for unfinished business with Mama! If so, Glenn had a tight rope on her. I hoped a haint could be restrained with a rope! He continued to pull the body up a hillside where the dreadful moans hushed. He dug a hole where pea vine covered the ground and green grass grew boot-top high. The spot sorta looked like cow heaven.

Dad came into the house with ruffled feathers. "Well, Cleo, you got your wish. I just buried $150. Guess you can pan store-bought milk for gold; it costs high." Mama said, "She won't kick nobody else!" She showed no remorse, even making up a riddle about it.

> *"Down in the barn yard, two sticks*
> *That old cow has four tits.*
> *Every time you squeeze one,*
> *She kicks."*

Dad walled his eyes in disgust, counted the loss, and bought another cow.

Mama had little time for aggravation and hindrances to her heavy daily chores.Each Monday was set aside for washing clothes. Mama was cleaner than a hound's tooth, boiling everything from socks to hair bows. She made us constantly wash our hands with plenty of soap because she knew the dangers of germs.

Granny Lou remarked, "I'd drink milk strained

through a sock if Cleo washed it." Strangers who asked directions to our house were told, "Just go t' where the whitest clothes are hanging out."

Early in the morning after the dishes were washed and scalded in the boiling metal dishpan on top of the stove, the beds made, and the house swept, she began bailing water from the spring filling two cast iron pots that sat kind of crooked in a crude rock furnace near the spring box. She might ask for help starting the furnace fire. If the wood was wet or burned slowly she remarked, "That wood wouldn't burn in hell with the blowers on it." After the process was started she would not allow anybody "dabblin' in her washin'." As the water heated, large loads of laundry were toted to the porch and sorted into large galvanized tubs. A ribbed rub board and plenty of Octagon soap were used for the first cleaning process.

She believed in lots of Clorox, but never bought it on sale. "There must be somethin' wrong with sale stuff, else they wouldn't be tryin' to get rid of it. It might be "watered down". Each scrubbed piece of apparel left soapy tubs into the boiling pots for thirty minutes. She used a white stick to lift steaming pieces into rinse water. Rinsing was not complete until the water was crystal clear. After she cleaned the clothesline with a bleach soaked cloth, she made individual trips back and forth with tightly wrung out apparel to the clothesline.

Dazzlingly white clothes hung in perfect order gently moved by a mid- morning breeze. In the winter, her fingers froze to the metal line. Pieces of skin stayed attached. She never complained unless the blood stained the piece she was working on.

One day Dad bought an electric pink and white wringer-type washing machine that sat on the back porch until a neighbor (when he was sober) built a tiny gray concrete block building near the spring. It was complete with a new furnace made of rocks from the creek bed. He also built a flue that "would draw your drawers off." A flue without a good draft will fill the house with smoke. He installed the luxury of running water and electricity. Just inside the door were twin silver rinse tubs alongside the pretty pink and white washing machine.

I was playing with pie plates near the white rose bush Mama had rooted from Grandma McConnell's grave. She passed on from cirrhosis of the liver when I was two years old. Roses comforted Mama without words when she cried over fond memories. They were in full bloom. Mama could lighten any moment with humor. "We've got two kinds of bloomers: some on the line, some on the bush."

The wind embedded soft perfume into hanging fabrics drying in the sun. Sister Bea was jerking a rope tied to the clothesline to scare bugs off the laundry. If one lit on the wash, Mama jerked it down to wash again.

Suddenly, our attention was grabbed by a loud, shrill scream. It was akin to mountain panthers, roaming on mountaintops seeking prey in dark woods. The high-pitched sound kept coming. My heart jumped about like I'd swallowed a bucking horse. Emotions erupted like exploding volcanoes. IT WAS MAMA! Bea was first responder. Lunging through the narrow door, she found Mama stuck to the pink and white washing machine.

"ELECTROCUTION!" hollered Dad as his long legs cleared the yard. Chickens scattered like a storm was rising. Then, "Lord, do help us!" as he passed by the rose bush. A very young Bea barely managed to reach the electric box, disconnecting the power cord. Mama fell to the wet gray concrete like a limp dishrag, but alive.

Quickly, Dad scooped her up into his big arms. Running towards the pick-up truck, he yelled, "Go stay with Granny Lou!" No grass grew under his feet. We watched as spinning tires sifted sand. The ford waters were knocked dry as the pickup cleared the creek speeding towards the hospital. The doctor said she was lucky to be alive as he signed admission papers.

Kids under twelve years old were not permitted hospital visits, so we never saw Mama for weeks. Time stood still as we waited. Granny Lou was confident Mama would return. Sure enough, one afternoon we spied a passenger with Dad in the pickup truck nearing the ford waters. We watched from Granny Lou's porch to see who it was. It was MAMA!

We all leaped from the porch onto the ground. Ernest outran Bea and me through the pasture, sliding underneath the gate like a baseball player. We nearly knocked her down with hugs. She was all black and blue. Her arms and legs were swollen like the black stovepipes in the kitchen. She jested, "Darkness settled on me and I can't wash it off. Look how fat I got in the hospital!"

At the end of the day, the last songbird hushed. The moon hung overhead like a big bright pearl. The stars pinned back a jeweled roof over Kelly's Creek. The only sound was the slow crackling of the dying fire. A holy hush fell, the kind you only expect on Christmas Eve. Mama was home. We were grateful. Dad said, "All right, younguns, kneel down and let's thank the good Lord." He talked to God like He was sitting in the straight chair among us.

If you want to test your faith, pull up an empty chair and talk to God.

Years later Dad bought Mama an automatic washing machine. We laughed when she asked, "Where do you build the fire? You can't boil clothes in an automatic washing machine."

"A THREEFOLD CORD IS NOT QUICKLY BROKEN"
Ecclesiastes 4:12

Our community embraced one another as family. Union is strength and a secret to mountain sufficiency.

Mama held one account especially precious. Long before I was born, my oldest brother, Edward, was stricken with diphtheria and scarlet fever at a very young age. Mama recalled, "We ran for the doctor." He said, "That baby looks like he's been hit in the head with a hog ax. If he makes it until morning, he might have a chance."

Our neighbor, Pearl Chastain (and she was a pearl), was making biscuits when word of need fell on her ears. Traces of flour remained on outstretched hands as she came through my parents' door. Love never considers being exposed to contagious diseases. She rolled her sleeves up ready for service. Mama and Aunt Mary were in the sick room, applying heavy coats of Vaseline that prevented the scarlet fever scales from spreading.

Miss Pearl made onion poultices for his feet and kept potato slices on his forehead. Vinegar-soaked towels layered his small hot body. When his fever reached dangerous levels, they soaked him in tubs of cool water beside his bed.

Eight long days turned into eight longer nights, but all stood strong, especially in prayer. The number "eight" means new beginnings, multiplied by two is sixteen, which means love.

Mama said, "When the fever finally broke,

Edward turned as black as coals in the fireplace, just like he was burned out with no more fire to fight. We thought we'd lost him. He was the picture of death, eating soda crackers. Edward finally cried. We cried too, for joy. I will always be grateful to Miss Pearl and Aunt Mary who stood strong with me".

Neighbors like Miss Pearl are life-giving medicines without price. They are the warmth that melts killing frosts.

Three cords lying side by side are of equal strength, but braided together they become one cord. Strong cords of faith drive doubt from our hearts when we unite in love with one mind and one accord. The Ultimate strength manifests through HIS people.

Hog-butchering days were another example of how the community came together. Uncle Earl Holt was a master at the whole process. He and others gathered at mountain homes in November when the weather stayed cold enough to keep meat from spoiling.

Dad knew how to make a pig's tail curl, always raising two fat hogs. Days before the event, he squinted over dingy pages in Grier's Almanac, looking for the right signs. "Don't ever kill a hog on the new moon because the meat will shrink. There won't be enough lard to grease the gun barrel." Slaughtering on a full moon ensured much grease and better meat.

I detested slaughtering days, doing all I could to avoid the bloody sights and sounds of axes chopping meat into sections for canning, curing, or giving away to others.

One cold November afternoon, dark skies spit blue snowflakes as brother Ernest and I rushed off the school bus. We ran up the road, hurrying towards the fireplace. I never suspected butchering activity had been moved into the house because of the cold. We ran headlong into white, hairless, blood-streaked hogs lying in front of the roaring fire. I fainted "dead'r" than four o'clock.

Occasionally, someone gave us beef. One winter Dad was going to hold a bull while its owner hit it in the head with a hammer. The fellow was very cross-eyed. Dad asked, "Do you always hit where you look? If you do, get somebody else to hold this bull."

It's funny how family bonds work. We will fight and scrap with each other then fight others for each other. Brother Ernest is two years older than me and was a master at instigating conflict.

Name meanings originate from languages. The meaning often bears the nature of a person. "Ernest" means battle. He is two years older than I am and like a burr under a horse saddle. Mama said, "Poison ivy will never bother that boy. I do declare he sugars his oatmeal with gun powder every morning." Demons seemed to dance in his brown eyes underneath a home crew-cut (haircut). A twisted hickory switch stayed within arm's reach, but had little effect. Mama whipped Ernest like "pattin" for a dance. He had A.D.H.D... XYZ... plumb off the page, squirming like a maggot in hot ashes unable to be still.

Brother
Ernest

Me

Sister Bea

Beatrice
(Bea) is four years younger than I am. We hardly
knew she was on the place until Ernest riled her.
"Beatrice" means voyager. Both meanings are true
to their nature.

Bea was the "Miss Prissy" type, occupying herself with paper dolls cut from old Sears catalogues
that she seated on arranged "church pews" made
from kindling sticks. She even passed the offering
plate and gave altar calls. When Bea grew tired of

playing church, Mama swept the mess into the fire. Bea chastised her paper dolls, "I warned every one of you where you were going if you didn't come to the altar." She often changed their apparel for ocean voyages or dressed them in skimpy bathing suits. Mama jested, "This must be from saint t' sinner day." Bea had Dad's chinquapin eyes that melted Mama's heart, managing to get just about anything she wanted. She was spoiled rotten.

A well-guarded shoulder bag usually hung down her side filled with costume jewelry, nail polish, and hair combs, which she could not get through extremely curly hair. Adornments of thin metal strips cut from old Prince Albert tobacco cans crimped on Bea's head. She looked like Buckwheat on the "Little Rascals" television show. A full-blown battle erupted when Ernest jerked that bag away.

My name, "Barbara", means stranger. I get good mileage from that. I ain't no preacher, but the Apostle Paul said, "Be good to strangers. They might be angels unawares." I do my share of "harpin" and "flappin" when my feathers get ruffled.

One cold January afternoon Mama began to discern weather signs. The chimney smoke settled close to the ground and the fire was making "trompin" sounds like boots swishing deep snow. Raising a cup of water to her mouth, she said, "I can taste snow in th' spring water. The stock was laying down this morning around the barn. Yes sir, a doozy of a snowstorm is a'comin'. If we can't make it to the outhouse, we'll just have to pee in the gun barrel and shoot it out the window." We laughed as clouds gathered and excitement swelled. Sure enough that night, large snowflakes descended from Heaven, covering our world with blankets of white purity. It settled on every branch, twig, and limb. Small noses withdrew from windowpanes in morning's light to go gather new snow from locust fence posts. We hoped Mama would make us delicious snow cream. After a few rounds of snowball fights and a couple of snow angels, a glimpse of something pink caught my attention.

I drew near to investigate. To my horror, my only baby doll, "Nancy Louise", the one Santa brought just a month ago was lying face down in the cold snow and NAKED! Quickly, I grabbed the doll by bare feet. Her soft hair was now a crew cut! A full, black beard and mustache were drawn with a fire coal on her rosy face. I guess this was the first sex change to come to the mountains!

Ernest took refuge in the house, watching and snickering from the frosted window as he warmed by the fire. When I entered the house, he said, "I hope she gets sick and dies." In a fury, I lunged into him, shoving him backwards, seating him squarely down on the blazing back stick in the fire. Sudden sounds of straight chairs crashing to the floor vibrated through the room as Dad and Sister Betty pulled Ernest to safety. Smoke from blazing britches filled the house. Luckily, he was wearing long johns and was not injured. Once the fire was extinguished on my brother, Dad started one on me.

As kids, we entertained ourselves in many

ways. Crude boards, rusty nails, weak ropes, and wobbling wheels came together for a reckless adventure. That death trap wagon was no comparison to the wrath of Mama after we cut donuts in the ash pile, sending clouds of gray and black dust onto her clean laundry hanging on the clothesline.

We carved pistols and swords from soft wood scraps. Toy cars were made from paper matchboxes and driven on roads in clay banks. Green leaves served as money for gasoline pumped from old hosepipe ends. Plastic bottles and Clorox jugs turned into roadside farm animals. Soap boats bubbled in the creek underneath small flutter mills made from routed corn stalks that piped the water to turn the mill. We made darts from corncobs; chicken feathers stuck into the soft pith guided them to target. A forked ivy stick, inner tube strings, and a piece of leather became slingshot weapons. The woods were filled with old tire swings and tree houses.

Ernest chased me about the yard with spring lizards and crawfish. A mountain superstition warns that if a crawfish pinches you, it won't let go until it thunders. It wasn't cloudy when he did this. He tied rock-filled cans to stray dog tails; each time the can hit the ground, the dog ran faster to get away. Homer, the cat, was terrorized with paper tails and booties. We watched a "cat show". When Homer grew tired or dizzy, he just collapsed. Ernest would say, "He ran out of gas."

Apples were thrown from the orchard with stick spears. Strays went over Mama's clothesline. She came out the door with the twisted switch behind her back. Ernest ran into the woods. She said, "All right, young man, you will have to sleep sometime." At night she settled all debts.

One day Ernest threw eggs on the porch screen. She dashed a bucket of water on him. He retaliated with half a bushel of black walnuts right through the screen door. She called Dad home; he locked him in the smokehouse. Ernest tore the door off.

FINALLY, Dad bought him a bike from the Western Auto Store. Ernest laced the wheel spokes with shiny can flips that glistened in the sun. Strips of heavy plastic extended through the spokes creating a motorcycle sound. Neighborhood kid Nelson Miller got a bike too. They stayed gone all day riding. The bike kept him busy and us sane.

\

My Beloved Granny Lou

Nancy Lular Harkins was born to Sarah Parker and John Harkins in Buncombe County, North Carolina, August 5, 1887. She was my Dad's mother, and my guardian angel. Everyone called her "Granny Lou" because midwives were called granny women. She lived just above our house at pasture's edge in a small shack with fake-brick siding. Cornfields grew right up to the yard's edge. A pole fence surrounded the yard to keep out the cows' manure that she called "cow pocketbooks."

A small, rough porch extended over a huge rock. It was a wonderful sliding board, which, in turn, kept Mama busy sewing patches over tears in our worn-out breeches. I lurked for an opportunity to sneak underneath the pasture gate towards her abode to become her shadow all day.

I would make my way up shaky steps to an old screen door. Its holes were plugged with wads of cotton from aspirin bottles and favored a snowy Christmas card. A fly could have kicked it down and come on in. I grabbed the thread-spool knob and entered into the presence of my angel.

Her moon-shaped face and sharp cheekbones radiated with love, touching lives like pure dew on tender petals. A silver bun of shiny hair rested neatly on the top of her head, held in place with

Note the cotton balls in the screen.

small, white hair combs. She only let it down at night to wash and comb. It always smelled like Listerine. Words of wisdom and the law of kindness were in her mouth. She was a picture of contentment.

A homemade, tattered dress reached downwards, touching the tops of dusty shoes with holes cut in the sides to ease ailing corns. (Did you know angels get corns?) Tan, knee-high cloth stockings were held in place by elastic garters; she was against "bareleggedness." Light blue eyes, like pools of flashing water, were beginning to dim as she sat in a wooden chair struggling to thread needles. "They make these durn things smaller every year. Somebody peeped through my 'specs and stole the strength out of them."

Tiny hands could fit inside jelly jars with ease and pull piglets from lazy sows. They took eggs from under setting hens without ruffling a feather and plucked grapes and berries among thorns. She possessed a special touch that felt like God's own hand mending scrapes and scratches, making all things new. While in her company, I felt like the only person on earth who mattered.

During cropping season her hands wrapped around a splintered handle on a gooseneck hoe, scraping around Holcomb Prolific field corn. Corn was life. An old straw hat was held in place by tattered ribbons around her wrinkled chin, and sat on top of her silver hair vanished over the hilltop to row's end at creek side and reappeared at the beginning of the next row of corn. This continued until the war with weeds ended.

From the creek bank, she picked fragrant peppermint plants, stuffing them in a knee-length checkered apron. City folks used it to season drinks. She used it for stomach medicine and a teaching tool. Faint, sweet fragrance filled the air as she pulled mint leaves from her pockets, saying, "Let's make it mad." Then she rubbed the leaves briskly between her hands to produce a strong and powerful fragrance.

"In this life, sometimes we are crushed t' pieces and rubbed raw, but stay the course. Crushing will make you stronger. You will smell better, too."

Granny Lou knew what it was to endure life's crushing blows. Her mother died October 12, 1907 one year after Granny Lou married Ale Taylor. About five months before Dad was born, Grandpa Ale was injured at work. A heavy cog-wheel attached to a steam-powered engine became loose. Somehow it fell striking both his kneecaps. He died at home from a blood clot.

She received $500 from a Woodman of The World death insurance policy. After she paid his funeral bill, the remaining money was spent on sixteen acres of rough mountain land located on the headwaters of Kelly's Creek.

A finger-size trickle of crystal water seeps from underneath a huge rock surrounded by cooling green ferns high on the mountain where eagles nest and the red doe feeds on an abundance of acorns and green foliage. The headwater unites with other small tributaries flowing through rough mountain clefts. Moving waters merge together and blend with rustling sounds of the living forest. Harmonies of nature's voices speak without words, more desired than fine gold. Suddenly, white cascades spill over underlying rocks forming beautiful waterfalls. The force of the flowing, falling waters births a stronger, incorruptible voice. Water is symbolic of Divine nature. There is nothing like the sight and sound of many waters rushing downward. It speaks of power and cleansing. Rays of sun's reflection produce prisms of light like a million sparkling jewels framed by wild rhododendron blooming on the creek banks. The trees planted by the rejuvenating water are taller and stronger.

Secrets of the mountains are experienced near the voice of running waters blending with night crickets and cool breezes, passing through unlocked doors and open windows. Running water is symbolic of life and change. Standing waters will stagnate. Mountain people are like small branches, feeding into a larger community of many waters.

Kelly's Creek from my back yard

Kelly's Creek is home to rainbow trout swimming in clear, shallow pools of freedom un-vexed by baited hooks. The name "Kelly" means "descendant of war." Without ever knowing that, when a minor squabble broke out my folks laughed and said, "If you live on Kelly's Creek you better learn how to fight."

After Grandpa Taylor died, Granny Lou moved into an old log house on Kelly's Creek with her widowed father, John Harkins, to raise Dad and his three sisters, Oshie, Mae and Mary. Her father was a mountain peddler specializing in Indian herbs.

John Harkins
1865 - 1953

She was widowed eight years before marrying Julius Elisha Thomas in 1925. Grandpa Julius was a widower with five children. Dad was eight years old and excited to have stepbrothers. Grandpa Harkins told Dad he did not have to move with Granny Lou when she left to a new home, but if he did, he could not come back. "It ain't what you think it is; Julius Thomas is a stern man."

One day Grandpa Julius sent Dad and his stepbrother John to the field to work the corn. On the way they stopped by the old barn to kill rats with rocks. Grandpa Julius appeared and said, "I told you to go the field, not to kill rats." He picked up a piece of rusty barbed wire and cut their backs with many lashes. Later he threatened to fill the wounds with salt. Their blood soaked shirts enraged Granny Lou and Dad's sister Aunt Mary who was about thirteen years old. Aunt Mary slept with an iron pipe underneath her bed vowing never to allow Grandpa Julius to hurt anyone else. People said he had "spells." Perhaps the dreadful abuse only happened once. I never saw that side of him. He was good to Granny Lou. I loved him for that alone.

Grandpa Julius Elisha Thomas

When I was young, six days a week at exactly 11:00 in the mornings, he walked by our house dressed in matching Duck Bill work clothing enroute to the mailbox about half a mile away. His posture and strides were perfect. His steel gray eyes usually were hard focused, not looking to the left, nor the right as he stepped along the roadside. Underneath long sleeved shirts were white cuffs of long johns that he wore year round, saying, "What will keep out the cold, will keep out the heat."

His face was stern and fixed as if in deep thought. Sometimes he closed his eyes and listened to moving winds rustling orchard trees until dark clouds appeared overhead. Thunder jarred the house and lightning bathed Kelly's Creek in light. Grandpa Julius was unmoved by storms but studied raindrops on shaking windowpanes trickling downward. Nothing rattled his cage, not even broken fences letting the cows in the corn.

He had Samson-like strength. Bulls in nearby pastures let him pass peaceably without a challenge. Grandpa Julius made quick work of troublemakers. Once, a neighbor asked him to come tame an unruly drunk who had whipped two grown men. He grabbed the drunk man's swinging arms and tied him to a tree until he sobered up.

Before he made journeys on foot five miles to town, he would break and drink three raw eggs in a bowl, saying, "They make me long winded." He carried house goods on his back and two hundred pounds of cow feed on his strong shoulders. He made non-stop round trips to town twice a month. Somehow he managed to tuck two bottles of Orange Crush soda into his sack. We shared those bottles sitting on a big rock in the pasture surrounded by moss and flowers. Occasionally, he shared folk songs and riddles:

"What's round as a saucer, deep as a cup, the Mississippi River can't fill it up?" (a sifter)

"What has a head, but cannot think? (a nail)

"What is round as a ball, sharp as an awl, lives in the summer dies in the fall? (chestnut burr).

"Once it was green and growing, now it is dead and singing." (a fiddle)

"What goes to the water but cannot drink? (cowbell)

"Four stiff standers, four down hangers, two lookers, two crookers, and one switchabout? (a cow)"

Each Sunday morning he went to the Baptist

church. Sometimes I'd watch him primp in front of a small mirror hanging on a rough pine wall. His face shined after a close shave topped off with baby oil patted on a front bald spot. Carefully he turned up a white collar to put a colorful tie in place. I asked, "Why do you wear those?" He said, "To keep my feet warm."

He coveted knowledge and read everything he could. When he was a child he walked from his mountaintop home to the one room schoolhouse on Kelly's Creek. "I jumped from sun spots to sun spots to keep warmer," he told me.

I asked, "Why didn't you just stay home by the fire? "Because a cat curled up by the fire can't read."

An old Blue Back Speller by Noah Webster rested underneath a worn Bible close by his resting place at the end of a small couch. Sometimes he turned to the fable chapter in the blue book and read stories like this to me:

The Bear and the Two Friends

"Two friends, setting out together upon a journey which led through a dangerous forest, mentally promised to assist each other, if they should happen to be assaulted. They had not proceeded far, before they perceived a bear making toward them with great rage.

"There were no hopes in flight; but one of them, being very active, sprang up into a tree; upon which the other, throwing himself flat on the ground, held his breath and pretended to be dead; remembering to have heard it asserted that this creature will not prey upon a dead carcass. The

bear came up and after smelling of him some time, left him and went on. When he was fairly out of sight and hearing, the hero from the tree called out, "Well, my friend, what said the bear? He seemed to whisper you very closely." "He did so," replied the other, "and gave me this good advice, never to associate with a wretch, who, in the hour of danger, will desert his friend."

Grandpa Julius had lots of friends and fellow "chicken catchers." Several times a month a large truck came from nearby Dillard at six o'clock in the evening loaded with men and crates bound for nearby poultry houses to do a night's work. Grandpa Julius got on the truck. He could carry nine white hens that he crammed into crates. After the catchers finished they liked to watch Grandpa Julius dance for he was limber as a rag, never tiring after a night of hard work. He slept in daylight hours and pretty much kept to himself the rest of the time.

The landscape was heavy-laden with rocks and pesky roots with hungry claws deeply embedded in rich soil. (It is said fence posts sprout here, and to rid yourself of an enemy, plant fast growing vines underneath his bedroom window. They will choke them to death by morning.) No mortal hand could free the land. Mules and horses were vital aids.

Granny Lou was as rugged as the land she bought.

Granny Lou (L) and her sister, Aunt Lela

Granny Lou and I spent much time along the creek banks, hunting lizards for shade-tree fishermen. Sometimes in the summer she sat near the water knitting heavy wool socks. She sold these to moonshiners in the winter for fifty cents a pair. They favored our area because of necessary water and white corn needed to make "shine" under Granny Lou's watchfulness.

Her keen ears knew each vehicle, rounding the mountain coming towards her house. Usually, only four ventured our way: the school bus, mailman, Dad, and the moonshiners. A white sheet mounted on a long pole stood near her house. When she heard a strange-sounding engine rounding the mountain, she ran outside to grab that pole. I'd ring all the spare cowbells, as she waved a white flag frantically into the air. It was a signal to the moonshiners to hit the high country; the revenuers were coming! They were friends and trusted us. Did you know angels were watchers?

Bill Welch, one of my favorite shiners, drove an old panel wagon, loaded with white sugar, corn, and Mason jars. He was short and toothless, but grinned like a jackass eating briars. Laced, brown work boots showed traces of mash from his still. Baldness was exposed when he removed his hat to eat at Granny Lou's table. He jested, "I have t' tote my dandruff around in my hand." His voice was just above a whisper. Granny Lou said, "It's because shiners learn to be quiet. Take a lesson."

She knew the sound of Bill's panel wagon well. The shifting of gears revealed his approaching nearness. Granny Lou motioned with her hands for me to go open the pasture gate. I jumped off the big sliding rock to struggle with heavy sourwood gate poles.

The gas pedal met the metal floorboard as he

approached. Granny Lou said, "Bill crawls in the carburetor all th' way to the hill top; he lets the rough side drag." The panel wagon's body looked like a low rider pressed near the ground from heavy loads of liquor-making materials. Black smoke poured from the exhaust, mixing with white steam underneath the hood as he cleared the ford waters wide open. He fought the steering wheel like a bear with his right hand. The other was throwing bananas, apples, and candy out the window. Goodies landed at my feet like those thrown by Santa Claus in a Christmas parade. Granny Lou knitted the stockings; Bill brought the stuffers.

There were several production sites operating near our house on government property. When feuds broke out between the moonshiners it was best to wear a kettle over your head when you went to the mailbox.

Shine customers would cross hell on a rotten log to get it. Granny Lou doctored with it or started fires. Several times, the cows changed denominations and partook of mash boxes. They wobbled to the barn. Dad thought they were poisoned on wild cherry. It was the smell that told on the happy cows. The milk tasted funny for days.

Early one fall morning, Dad hitched Kate, the white mule, to a small farm cart, gathering corn drying in the fields. It was favored by moonshiners for the best pure whiskey, but Dad ground it into grits, meal, and animal feed. The quiet of the morning was suddenly interrupted by a loud blast! Bright colors streaked the mountainside like a bad lightning storm. The revenuers had slipped up the backside of the mountain with dynamite and blown up a still. The blast scared the mule. She fell down between the cart shaves, trembling. Dad thought they'd killed Kate. We heard sledgehammers shattering cases of half-gallon Mason jars for about an hour. Granny Lou mourned each crash of glass. "They don't have to be s' greedy and bust good cannin' jars." Somehow the shiners escaped. Scents of beer and liquor drifted down Kelly's Creek. Granny Lou hid and guarded her jug of "medicine" from the revenuers.

She worked alongside the late, beloved Dr. Lester Neville, absorbing all she could do to help others. He was a medical wizard, possessing great knowledge of healing herbs growing among us planted on the mountainside by the Great Physician. Dr. Neville's skill and kindness exalted him. In his care, faces of pain became those of peace. His picture hung in our house simply because it made Dad feel better. Granny Lou said, "The Lord makes all kinds of medicine and knowledge to use them. The work of a doctor never ends."

Boneset plants (perennial daisies) grew along roadsides and fields bowing their blooms low for easy pickings. They were used for many ailments such as flu and pneumonia. Granny Lou claimed boneset was good for arthritis. Yellow Root is a most bitter herb. I cringed at a dose for stomach aches. Granny Lou said, "It will kill ye r' cure ye." Muscle spasms and stress were treated with yellow Lady Slippers, a wild orchid that resembles a small moccasin. It is rare to find these today because people dig them and take them away hoping to domesticate them. Wild herbs once plentiful, have become scarce because of the ready cash offered for them.

Upper, Lady Slipper • Lower, Ginseng

Pokeroot poultices were thought to draw pain from bodies. Salty fatback (pork) had a drawing effect on poison and swelling from bee stings, particularly "packsaddles." Packsaddles are bees that hide in corn shucks. Their stings are especially painful. Colds were doctored and tonsils swabbed with Gilead salve. Jeremiah, the prophet, spoke of this balm: "Is there no balm in Gilead? Is there no physician there? Why then is not the health of the daughter of my people recovered?" Bible symbolism was understood by Granny Lou. She knew God is the real healing balm. The divine gift of true faith healers will never be exploited by dancing under a tent or passing plates for money. They are laborers of love.

Granny Lou dropped all her work when a midwife's service was needed in the community. Nervous husbands appeared at her door in all weather and all hours. Picking up a small satchel stocked with towels, scissors, dressings, catnip tea, and a Bible, she left for days to attend expectant mothers and dress newborn babies. Payment of eggs, clothes, or vegetables was enough for helping others. On returning, the satchel and contents were washed in hot soapy water before baking in the oven to kill any germs.

We were too young to know where babies came from. Sex was never mentioned except in terms that had no connection. I was told Dr. Neville caught me in an eight-pound lard bucket near the cabbage patch. He was tuckered out chasing me, a real ridge runner. When Mama birthed younger sister Bea, "She ordered her from a catalogue." Granny Lou said, "A buzzard laid your brother,

Ernest, on a stump, and the sun hatched him out." I believed her.

During mating season, the cows were "bullin'". They went crazy then, running the fence line, bawling and pawing the dirt. Often they jumped the fence "to go to town." If one mounted another, we were told, "Ahh, she's just tarred (tired) of walking." The roosters were just being "cocky" or "whippin'" the hens.

In August, Granny Lou swapped her long dress for overalls and borrowed a pair of boots from Grandpa Julius to enter into the blackberry patches. The boots were greatly oversized and arrived at her destination before she did. Mama said, "Here comes the boots. Granny Lou will be on after while."

She gathered berry buckets and a gooseneck hoe, which doubled as a walking stick and snake prod around clustery vines. "Don't play with snakes; go for th' head. When you enter the field, be armed, else you are buzzard bait for the enemy." Hay baling strings were soaked in kerosene oil and tied around ankles to ward off chiggers and bugs. Green grasshoppers sprang up in tall sage fields, spitting tobacco juice on us. Fat birds flew and fussed in tangled bushes because we plundered their food source. "Don't ever tear down a bird nest. If you do, the mama bird will hunt you down. You will hear a rapid pecking upon your windowpane late at night. She will cry tears of blood and say, 'You stole my wee, wee nest. You stole my wee, wee nest.' If she can get inside, she will peck your eyes out and fill the holes with droppings for breaking up her home.

When you go outside, she will swoop down on your head and take hair strands for her next nest. You will go crazy and wander these hills, slobbering like a mad dog. So think twice before you harm nature."

Clusters of luscious plump berries hung among many sharp thorns. Granny approached the task with study and caution, as if confronting a mad cat with dangerous claws. Impatience drew blood. "Handling berries is like dealing with people. There is good fruit in thar', but you have t' reach through thorns to gather the good. Thorns have purpose."

I ain't no preacher, but the Apostle Paul was given a thorn to keep him humble. I reckon that's a nice way of saying a pig from hell bothered him. We all have somebody like that to test our mettles and make us stronger.

Soon the buckets were filled and rounded over like purple hats. Our fingers and lips were purple, too. Blue fingers are a sign of low blood. Granny Lou jested, "We'll have t' dose up on iron when we get back home." She hoisted me onto small, but strong shoulders for a ride back home. I patted the shiny, silver hair bun like a horse. Huffing and puffing up the hills, she sang:

"The old gray mare,
She ain't what she used to be,
Ain't what she used to be,
Many long years ago."

We stopped to rest under aged trees with thick boughs bending near the earth. She picked and wove together green glossy leaves, fashioning a small head crown. Blue and crimson wildflowers served as jewels. This natural creation seemed to have a touch of magic for a queenly youngun. Sometimes she caught June bugs (metallic green beetles with wings). Strings tied to prickly legs made dandy toy airplanes, especially when the strings crossed and they crashed, only to take to the air again until she turned them loose.

I helped Granny Lou wash and look the fruit over for twigs. The berries were placed in a large pot to boil for juice. Then the juice and sugar were measured carefully and mixed for jelly. There was no such thing as store bought pectin. She tested the gelling perfection with a saucer dipped in the hot mixture. When three drops of purple juice ran into one big drop, the jelly was ready to pour into jars.

Cooling jars made popping sounds when they sealed. She raised thankful hands of praise saying, "Thank th' Lord, another one sealed, another one saved." Some of the berries became blackberry cobbler. She winked as we ate it. "Be careful none of that splatters on your noggin; your tongue will slap your brains out tryin' to get to it."

Granny Lou learned rich Indian customs from her grandmother, a full-blooded Cherokee Indian. They lived in White County, Georgia, during the Civil War years. Grandpa Parker was a veteran of the War. Granny Lou told me war stories passed down through generations: "Grandpa Frank was about thirty years old when he and all other men that were worth account in White County joined the 65th Regiment to fight in the Civil War. There was nothing civil about it. My mother was about five years old when he left for Service, but remembered the hard times. The Yankees stopped all supply routes, so women and children had to attend the fields and do all the hunting for survival. Imagine scraping dirt off smoke house floors to boil for salt, or using parched rye or corn for coffee substitutes."

The Confederate government started monthly rationing. Wagons loaded with cornmeal arrived to lines of women and children waiting for food. Granny Lou proudly spoke of two aunts who could not wait for designated days because the children were starving. They armed themselves with wooden mauls to meet the meal man. He was unwilling to allow them an early portion. Aunt Sally drew her heavy maul, daring him to move, while Aunt Nancy knocked the lock off the wagon door, swung inside, measured out only their portion, and left.

I asked Granny Lou if robbing the meal wagon was a sin. She said, "Not much of one; it would have been a greater wrong if they let the children die while keeping the law." She was proud to be named after Aunt Nancy.

Grandpa Frank wrote a few letters home, telling that his company was falling out like flies from scarlet fever and diphtheria. Winters were hard and the men slept on cold ground or in the wet mud. Food was scarce. He wrote that a buddy got his brains blew out on the battlefield. They splattered onto Grandpa's cornbread. He had no choice but to clean it up and eat it—that or starve to death. He wrote that his breeches (pants) were stiff with blood and could stand up by themselves. He saw heaps of dead men stacked like butchered hogs. Rotting flesh tainted the air as their pocket watches ticked time.

Headstone Frank Parker

During the Civil War days, the family cabin was burned to the ground in White County by a mob of mean boys. Aunt Nancy saw from a distance the boys roping and tying the schoolteacher. He had returned from the war. They said he mistreated them before leaving for battle. Aunt Nancy approached the gang and heard their intention to hang him. She tried to talk them out of the evil deed, but they had blood in their eyes. She was far outnumbered by the raging gang.

When the teacher became missing, the community started asking questions. Aunt Nancy told what she saw. The boys invaded her home to kick, stomp and threaten her. It was nearly dark when she ran through the cornfield to escape their attack. She could hear approaching boots searching each row for her. They came so close the dust stung her eyes, but she escaped. "Their misconduct started with stealing eggs. When neighbors reported one boy to his mother for correction, she took him in a back room where she kept an old black trunk. She told the boy to jump up and down screaming, as she beat that old trunk. That would appease the listening crowd outside. Well, later he was caught and convicted of murder. Now at the gallows, he said, 'Mother, if you had beat me instead of that old trunk, I might not be here today.' That's the plumb truth."

Stories and tales are kept alive and passed from generation to generation.

The news of Aunt Mary, Granny Lou's daughter, and Uncle Valley John Carpenter visiting for the day excited me. She was a walking fun factory filled with wit, games, and stories that kept me spellbound for hours.

A sure sign of their soon arrival was extra coffee grounds taken from Granny Lou's red Luzianne bucket. Extra measure causes the coffee to be guilty of being coffee. It looked like perked syrup pouring from the pot. "If you can read a newspaper through it, it ain't coffee. It's skeered water." After Aunt Mary's family arrived, we all drug up straight chairs around the fire. The grown-ups saucered the black gold and talked.

Aunt Mary: "Grandpa Harkins wuz a travelin', fiddle-playing peddler. He went lot a' places peddlin' Indian herbs. One time he was at a mule sale in Buncombe County, North Carolina, near the Smoky Mountains. There was this feller standing next t' him with only one arm. Grandpa said, "Mister, if ye don't mind me asking, how'd ye lose your arm?"

The feller says, "Well, I'll tell ye; I wuz bear huntin' deep in the mountains. It wuz rainin' with thick fog. You could stick your finger in it and leave a hole. The woods wuz cold and slick. My dogs struck up an ol' she bear. I could hear them running hard, stopping occasionally for the fight. Finally, the sound came from a hollow that told me the dogs had her bayed. I rushed along the wet ground until we met up. My best dog come flying out of a gully, landin' about eight feet above me. Th' fur wuz a' flyin'. My dog shook himself off and went right back to th' fight. There wuz an old log across the gully. I intended to walk that log t' get a good shot at that old bear. The log was rotten. It broke, throwing me right in amongst 'em. Somehow, I managed to cram the gun barrel down the throat of that bear and she bit and chewed my arm. I wuz able to git my Barlow pocketknife out with my good arm and open it with my teeth. I cut and jabbed until she bled t' death. My dogs were drippin' blood and began to whine and lay down beside me. Finally they left me in the woods.

"My wife said she heard them whining and a-scratchin' at th' door. When she saw blood all over em', she fetched the boys. They hitched the steer t' th' sled. Th' dogs led them t' me. That's how I lost my arm."

That was a warm up story for many others that usually followed. "We lived in an old house one time. Ever' night after the candle went out, you could hear a horse stomping around that house. If I ain't a-settin' here, I've heard it many a time. One day Harv Brown's wife asked me, 'Mary have ye heard the big hoss yet?' I sure did; he'd stomp 'til I got up. I think he wuz tryin' t' tell me where his owner buried money. It wuz either where the hoss started trompin' or where he quit, 'r both. I've wanted to dig."

I asked Aunt Mary, "What if a haint pops up when you break the ground?" She said, "I ain't skeered of haints, cuz a haint can't haint another haint." Granny Lou winked at me with twinkling eyes, "Do you believe that? If you believe all you hear, then you can eat all you see".

According to Aunt Mary, "There are boogers, witches, and haints; then there are people. Th' Bible speaks of em' and that's enough for me t' know it. One time our cow went bad. The milk just looked like cottage cheese when I tried to strain it. Granddad Carpenter said, "I can tell ye what's th' matter. Somebody has a grudge against ye and has bewitched that cow. You have t' break the spell. Go home and fix up a churn. Put a silver dime in the bottom. While th' milk clabbers, sweep th' house and put the broom under the doorstep. When you start churning on that silver dime, th' witch will come. If she steps over the broom, th' spell is broken. If she don't step over the broom, she will want to borrow three things. If you let her have 'em, the spell stays. So don't loan her nothing. And don't be surprised if you know the witch when she comes." Sure enough, as I churned a neighbor appeared. She wuz big and fat so it took effort for her to swing over the banister dodgin' th' hidden broom. I just kept on a-churnin'. Sure enough she asked to borrow three things. I made up my mind t' be fresh out of anything she wanted. After she left th' milk cleared up. Now that's th' sure enough truth, believe it 'r not."

I must have believed her. After she left I checked under beds, behind doors, and in cornfields and barn for boogers, witches, and haints.

(Aunt Mary is featured in the Foxfire Book series.)

My Sentence Begins

In the fall of 1960, I began a twelve-year sentence called school. It was chiefly a long lesson in discipline. Those who endured school usually became successful workers. Mama tugged on my bed covers, awakening me with a rhyme:

> *Birdie with a yellow bill*
> *Hopped upon my window sill*
> *Cocked its shiny eye and said,*
> *"Ain't you ashamed, you sleepy head?"*

It felt good "deckin" out in new duds. Ernest and I walked down the road as Mama watched and waved from the porch. I kept looking back, hoping she would change her mind and call me back home. At 7:00 AM, the familiar sounds of the school bus motor rounding the mountain came into hearing. It moved slowly around the curves like a big yellow mountain lion on wheels. Squeaking brakes made eerie sounds. The dusty bi-fold doors opened. I entered the mouth of the lion.

Mr. Coleman, the driver, lived on Kelly's Creek, too. Gloved hands gripped a weather-cracked steering wheel. When he smiled, golden teeth glistened among pearly whites. Wow! Could everybody grow those for riding his bus? We unloaded between two red brick monuments at the entrance of a big matching brick building.

The smell of freshly cut grass on large playgrounds brought flashbacks of summer fun, running barefoot through nature's carpet in cool pastures. Stepping through the monuments, life turned into big red pencils, huge crayons, musty books, patent leather shoes and dresses. I would do seven years of time here.

Miss Louise McKinney was long-time ruling principal. She started teaching in 1936 at the ripe age of sixteen. She was careful with her appearance and "dressed fit t' kill" in Sunday go-to-meeting clothes. Seamed, nylon hosiery highlighted a professional look. She regularly adjusted dark bifocal glasses that framed eyes of authority, the kind God only gives to teachers. Her hair was tightly permed, the kind Mama warned us about if cooties (head lice) infested. "Cooties and kinks don't mix. The only remedy is kerosene oil and a match. You can't get a lice comb through a briar patch." Needless to say, Mama made us paranoid of anybody with kinky hair.

Student rumors were that Miss McKinney owned three paddles: a big canoe oar, an electric board, and one with holes bored in it. I would soon find out. Everyone feared her office, located beside the water fountain where frisky kids pushed for watering positions. That's where the butting started that landed me in her office. Late one afternoon, an older boy shoved me into the instructional green board and batten wall. I crammed a fist into his face. He began to cry and wipe a bloody nose, which brought Miss McKinney rushing to investigate. I had much time that evening to worry about my fate the next day.

Mama tried to help. "Wear this tight elastic

girdle. The paddle will just bounce off; it won't hurt s' bad." Dad was furious. "You have smutted our name. You've got another one coming!"

Early the next morning, I sat in class like a prisoner awaiting execution. The approaching sounds of Miss McKinney's shoes, striking wooden hallways, caused me to sink deep in my desk. The doorknob wiggled, and then opened. I saw the hemline of a black dress. She called my name. The frog in my throat crossed its legs; I could not swallow. My heart stopped. We walked down the longest hallway in my life. Heat waves of anger that could have melted the wax on the floor radiated towards me. She shuffled around a papered desk to sit down as she adjusted her bi-focal glasses. I prayed they would steam up, and she could not see me. Her face turned red, then purple, then red again. A strong lecture followed before she opened the bottom desk drawer to draw her weapon. Ten hard licks did not hurt half as bad as the breaking of elastic bands in the girdle. It felt like an army of wasps loose in my drawers. Mama was wrong!

Our elementary school was staffed with caring teachers. My first grade teacher was Mrs. Ethel Page. Cut flowers from her yard filled the room with sweetness to match her character. She hid pressed flowers in our tiny books to brighten stuffy days. A much-worn desk drawer was well stocked with raisins and apples she gave for rewards. Mrs. Page made it a point to brag on her class in everything we did. She was also the school dentist. Sometimes students with loose teeth appeared in the hallway outside her classroom. Mrs. Page stepped outside. We could hear small faint moans filtering underneath the closed door. Mrs. Page returned with a small blood streaked tooth to place in a brown paper towel awaiting the tooth fairy at the student's home. Drawing small heads near her warm bosom in warm embraces made tooth pulling easier.

She collected pretty pinecones that we filled with peanut butter. A red ribbon affixed to the top made a dandy bird feeder to take home for Christmas. Dad said it was the perfect example of the welfare system. We saved ice cream sticks that became gingerbread houses complete with gum-drops for Christmas lights and a horse corral. Old Reader's Digest books turned into small white Christmas trees. She made the covering with white moistened laundry powders decorated with glitter.

At night Mama read to us from books I brought home. One afternoon I left a book out-side. The dog chewed up school property. I was scared to go back to school. Ernest said, "Give ye' a quarter, if you tell Miss McKinney the dog took a lesson out of it." No deal.

Miss McKinney enforced a strict dress code forbidding girls to wear pants or pant suits. Dresses were a must. She simply believed boys ought to be boys and girls ought to be girls. Bea got in trouble for wearing pants. In those days teachers did not pick up a phone to call parents when problems arose. Miss McKinney had a well-stocked closet to accommodate anyone who trans-gressed the rule. One harsh winter she allowed the girls to wear pants underneath a dress.

Each week Miss McKinney took a Sunday school attendance count that was announced each Friday during chapel. She played the piano as all students marched into a large room filled with gray folding chairs. She arose from the piano bench with an opened Bible. We had church for an hour. Because of her Christian efforts many children memorized Bible passages and can still recite them word for word. The Christmas story recorded in Luke chapter two and many Psalms come to mind, word for word just like they are written. Her efforts planted good words in our hearts instead of just our ears.

Many years after first grade teacher, Mrs. Page, retired I visited her in a brick home in the Wolffork community. It was decorated in the tradition of a born teacher displaying student memories on walls. She never forgot a single student and remembered something of interest about each one. She kept student papers in a box. She shared a letter sister Bea had written to her expressing her love. I asked Mrs. Page if I might have it. She said, "Why, no, Bea wrote it to me." Bea was very fond of her first grade teacher because Mrs. Page petted her rotten. Bea said, "When she couldn't promote me to second grade because I was too young, Mrs. Page set me in her lap and said, 'I am going to keep you with me another year.' I asked, 'Why?' She never bothered with reasons I could not understand. Her answer put to rest all sadness, 'Because I love you.' Instead of feeling like a failure, I felt honored to stay another year."

Many of my elementary school teachers have passed on to their reward. The old school building was sold to the city of Dillard and became city hall as well as our voting precinct. One year after we cast ballots, a fellow classmate stood outside chewing on a cigar butt as we reminisced about our school days. He said, "I can sense Miss McKinney somewhere in the shadows watching us." He turned to crush out his cigar. "It just don't taste the same here."

The Old Dillard Elementary School
Now, City Hall

Rabun Gap Nacoochee School

To Everything There Is A Season

Autumn voices carried by fall-scented winds usher in ordained change. Nature teaches and prepares the earth and her dwellers for cold seasons. Forest trees, once arrayed in nature's splendor, now have no shade for the weary, no fruit to bear.

Trees fulfill a purpose. Their deep, strong root systems hold mountains together. Leaves blanket the earth with soft protection, covering and teaching us. Biblically, men are likened to trees. Sometimes we stand barren in God's pasture, as cold winds pelt winter storms tossing our spirit; yet there is life in a barren tree. Cold seasons are vital for survival.

Dad said, "The Lord gives three signs before He calls our number: snow on the roof, windows on the eyes, and a cane in the hand."

By 1966, Granny Lou's silver hair had turned a snowy white. She already had specs and a cane. She moved much slower in the fields carrying home sacks of potatoes, onions, and apples that she rested on cool clay cellar floors. She strung cream-colored beans called "leather breeches" that hung drying from the rafters. Vacant tables held drying fruits, covered by white sheets to protect them from drunkards (fruit flies). Scented winds filtered through wigwam corn shucks, and white "roastin" ears filled the crib, waiting to be shucked and sorted.

"One for the dodger, (bread)
One for the feed,
One for the shiners,
One for seed."

Immediately after school, I would crawl underneath the pasture gate to sit at her side. She lay on a patchwork quilt draped over a vinyl couch, an uncommon sight. Her weathered face became sunken; her cheerful voice weak.

Grandpa Julius sat in his usual corner resting his eyes and nervously twiddled his thumbs. The church folks brought food and paper fans, advertising the funeral home. She chuckled, "Guess that's a dandy place to advertise for business." I gathered the herb pennyroyal from the pasture to stuff under mounds of pillows. She thought it helped her rest. Cancer has no mercy, nor respect of persons. Its ruthless, heinous fibers crept through my beloved's body like fast-growing kudzu plants in the summer.

In early October, when the leaves were in peak color, an ambulance took her away to the hospital. The dog began to howl near the spring box. I flung rocks at him. Howling dogs were a sign of death. Dad's chinquapin eyes blinked tears as our family loaded in the pickup truck to follow. At the hospital, a heart monitor chirped like a caged bird wanting to be free. Friends and neighbors crowded the waiting room and hallway. The air was thick with grief, like late fog in deep valleys that took its time to lift.

Sneaking by the nurse station, I entered the

intensive care unit and found my beloved inside a plastic oxygen tent. Her tiny hands were freezing from the ice buckets inside the tent. She was in a coma.

Granny Lou had taught me a song that flashed in my mind like crystal creek waters we were so fond of:

"I hold a clear title to a mansion
That Jesus has gone to prepare.
Fire cannot touch it,
Floods cannot harm it,
It never will need a repair.
The termites can't mar its foundation
For on the Rock of Ages it stands.
I feel that it's almost completed
And ready for me to move in."

Her last breath here was her first one in a perfect world.

Early the next morning, I took a long walk through a dried field, kicking the dirt in a blaming gesture. If ever fields were spoiled by sunlight, they were that day.

When you are a kid, those you love seem eternal. My heart was like her empty house. A dam of tears broke overflowing the pale in my soul. It felt like the universe clashed together, moving the stars out of their places. That is what it felt like to lose her to another world.

Neighbors gathered in the graveyard with shovels and mattocks. The church bell tolled her death. There was standing room only inside the church, with more people outside like leaves on the ground. The choir sang. Dry eyes were scarce. The air became chilled like silver sleet. The undertaker closed the coffin lid. I closed my eyes.

The days that followed felt dry and dusty. I wished for a magic moon to bring the blooms back. It took a long time for summer to return, but it did. I had to learn from the ordained cold season. Granny Lou never left me. She is hidden from fleshly eyes and among the great company spoken of by the Apostle Paul that helps us run our earthly race by cheering us on. She is the shower that melts into pure light and the white blanket of snow on blue-sifted hills. She is the new voice each season hovering over home.

Grandpa Julius remained on Kelly's Creek until his health failed. He lived with his daughters until his death in 1973.

Both Granny Lou and her mother passed on October 12

C oming north from Atlanta, drivers see this sign just after the Blue Ridge Divide that puts Rabun Gap on the map.

Unincorporated also defines most Appalachian people ungoverned by an organized world. Blinking drivers might completely miss our main attractions: Osage Farms, a post office, a small train museum, a Presbyterian church, and Rabun Gap-Nacoochee School founded in 1903 by the county's first college graduate, Andrew Ritchie. Dr. Ritchie had a passion to consolidate existing one-room schoolhouses scattered about the community and educate bright mountain minds. His first job of teaching was in my own community, Kelly's Creek. The one-room structure was called "Scuffletown." Dr. Ritchie struggled to expand his own education at Emory University and later, Baylor University. After he ran out of money, he learned from a pamphlet how a few students could work their way through school at Harvard University. This hands-on experience inspired him to offer a like work program in the founding of the school of his dreams, Rabun Gap-Nacoochee. One of two maple trees my parents bought from Dr. Ritchie to help support his efforts remain deeply rooted in their yard today.

The campus is stunningly designed, framing perfect mountain views over hundreds of acres of school-owned land. In the evening, chiming hymns serenade the community from a gold colored bell tower located on the main brick building, complementing rolling hay fields, red dairy barns, a gymnasium, dining hall and scattered dormitories that in my high school days housed about one-hundred boarding students The campus is immaculate, to say the least.

There was one government-operated high school in nearby Clayton during my high school years. It was severely overcrowded and could not accommodate an additional 140 students living in the north end of the county. Through an interesting and mutually beneficial arrangement, Rabun Gap-Nacoochee School operated as a normal public high school (grades 8-12) during the day, with government-provided teachers, principal, and administrative staff. Each weekday afternoon at 3:15 the school reverted back to being a private boarding school. Rules and regulations were strictly enforced on every aspect of boarding student lives during public school hours. This unusual arrangement provided a wonderful opportunity for community students to interact with about one hundred boarding students from different areas, cultures and backgrounds.

When I attended Rabun Gap-Nacoochee School, the Rabun Gap Presbyterian church occupied an entire wing of the school. There are long-standing ties between church and school.

Most of the school's faculty moved here from other areas. An exception was Mr. Stiles, science and biology teacher— a native of Rabun County who was born to teach. His love for teaching manifested through an amazing charisma. His slim frame dressed in sleek clothing moved among the students, involving us in all classroom activity. He didn't need a textbook; he was one. His knowledgeable lectures using mountain experiences mixed with humor kept us spellbound. They lasted far beyond homework assignments.

He was an avid sportsman who shared entertaining stories with us: "I was fishing in the river when I glimpsed the biggest trout imaginable swimming in an old sunken pickup truck. Attempts to cast through the window with well-baited hooks failed. Finally, I saw the problem (we waited with perked up ears.) Each time I cast my line that old trout grabbed the window knob and rolled it up."

Mr. Stiles kept us laughing a lot. A common mountain greeting is, "I haven't seen you in a coon's age." We learned how long that really was.

Displays of seeds, insects, and gems stimulated young minds. A gallon jar held a preserved pink pig immersed in formaldehyde. Then there were the days when biscuit pans with black dough bottoms, knives, and push pens were passed out. A huge bucket of preserved frogs followed. Granny Lou said, "Don't ever kill a toad-frog 'r your cow will give bloody milk." I suspected someone's entire dairy was going down.

The boys talked about how they could have provided sacks of fresh frogs from nighttime frog-gigging ventures. Teams gathered after dark around area ponds to listen for bullfrog croaks. Frogs are like families; they all talk at once. One boy shined a bright light, blinding the frogs, while another used the devil's own pitchfork to gig and bag the prey. Frog legs were then skinned to fry like fish. Mama forbid them in her kitchen. She said they made her nervous jumping around in the hot grease. (Another taboo was to never touch a flopping chicken fresh from the chop block. "All that quiverin' and shakin' will rub off on you.")

The girls cringed. Mr. Stiles laughed, "Dissecting frogs and clams are easy compared to college experience. Just wait until a load of slick alley cats is passed out. They look just like banana pudding inside." Needless to say, he got lots of extra pudding at lunch.

The boys continued their frog play, gouging out gray eyeballs to roll around on the countertop. Karen Cox, a boarding student, was unmoved, claiming the ability to eat them. Bets were laid on her words. Karen popped an eyeball in her mouth and swallowed. Mr. Stiles purposely offered no comfort. "I have never known anyone to survive eating eyeballs soaked in formaldehyde, but I have never known anyone to eat them. Fact is formaldehyde puckers the flesh; you could age fifty years in five minutes." Karen's rosy face turned a pale white. The class bell rang. She hopped out the door and up the stairway, but didn't croak.

Fifth period home economics class was a three-ring circus. The room was above the main hall. Lush hedge bushes lined the building. Birds flew back and forth, attending their nests. Dean of Students Don Arbitter enjoyed observing their activity on breaks from a lower office. One day Rethea Henslee and I threw hen eggs out the window. Large blobs of yellow yokes splattered near his shiny shoes. He looked at the eggs, then looked at the birds, then looked back at the eggs. We rolled on the floor, laughing as he scratched his head in wonderment. He hurried down the hall to find Mr. Stiles.

Another memorable teacher was Coach Cook, a fun but firm man, who also taught driver's education. The class was filled with experienced drivers. We could drive teachers up the wall and over the edge. One day Mr. Cook grew weary of competing for our attention. Our preoccupations were interrupted by loud sounds of crashing textbooks upon his wooden desk. He removed his glasses, wiping his face with both hands, as if to remove hot anger. "Y'all remind me of a bunch of cattle, heads lowered, swishing the tail, munching green grass, so unconcerned with anything else. Wasted words of instruction fall on deaf ears, which just might make life a little safer.

"I can talk to cows all day about heisting their tail, twirling it like a chopper, saving a few steps to the watering hole, hoping they might listen, but they never will, BECAUSE I CANNOT GET THEIR OR YOUR ATTENTION!"

He hit the nail on the head. Few classrooms held my attention.

As lovely as the surroundings were, I began to count the days to my sixteenth birthday and the freedom I would finally gain by quitting school.

I pondered Granny Lou's chicken lot. She did not clip their wings, yet they seemed content in their confined space. When she first cooped them, they tried a few times to fly out only to hit the wire fence, then give up. Mama despised chickens, "Chickens peck everything in front of 'em and mess on everything behind 'em. The best chicken is golden brown. Baptists have given them a hard time ever since a rooster told on Peter."

School kinda felt like a chicken lot. An invisible restrictive fence surrounded me. Only one brother, Edward, had worn Nacoochee's green and gold graduation attire. My other siblings seemed to be doing all right without a diploma. I suppose that is the nature of the unincorporated.

GLOWING IN THE DARK

Plans to quit school and find work had not changed. I chose journalism as an elective course in 1972, my junior year. Teacher Eliot Wigginton entered the classroom wearing a gray sweater, jeans, and work boots. "Eliot" is an uncommon name affixed to an uncommon man. His tall, lanky frame moved around collections of mountain artifacts as he found a student desk to sit in among us, not above us, a gesture that spoke volumes. Clear, sharp penetrating eyes surveyed each kid, looking for potential like an eagle looks beyond.

In 1966, "Wig" was fresh out of Cornell University with a Master's degree in teaching. His early journal records: "Last night, Rabun Gap called and definitely offered me a job-ninth-and tenth-grade English and one class of geography-all for $4,280 per year. One hundred-forty-plus kids, so I won't have time to write. They want me to live at the school. The worst part of the whole thing is that I think I just may take it. For a year, it might not be so bad-see what things are like down there as a teacher. I might really like it. I know I like the country anyway.

"I talked to Archie Ammons about it for a long time. He's one of the few professors here I feel I can talk to. He knows I've got job offers from Cleveland, New York, etc., but he says go to the mountains. My father doesn't want me to—it's less money, less security, less prestige, less chance for real success and advancement; but I'm still young. I can afford to take a flyer. I think I'll try it."

Wig was no stranger to the mountains. He had vacationed with his Dad at The Jay Hambidge Art Foundation located on seven hundred stunning acres near the school. Rolling landscapes and the sparkling waters of Betty's Creek afforded a young lad natural playgrounds. He never forgot the people who touched his life here. "It was Mary Hambidge's influence and Margaret Norton's honey cookies and cheese soufflés, Dean's quiet strength, and Claude Darnell's open friendship that brought me back." Wig became addicted to the secret of the mountains that abided within those who embraced him as family.

Rabun Gap-Nacoochee School principal, Morris Brown, hired Wig without an interview based solely on local recommendations. A phone call was placed from Rabun Gap to New York. Wig heard these words: "Come on down; Margaret says you are all right."

So, in the fall of 1966, Wig began his teaching career. In his own words from the introduction to *"The Foxfire Book"*: "About six weeks later, I surveyed the wreckage. My lectern (that's the protective device a teacher cowers behind while giving a lecture nobody's listening to) was scorched from the time Tommy Green tried to set it on fire with his lighter—during class. Charles Henslee had already broken off the blade of his Barlow knife in the floorboards. Every desk was decorated with graffiti. My box of yellow chalk was gone, and so were the thumbtacks that had held up the chart of the Globe Theater. The nine water pistols I had confiscated that very afternoon had been reconfiscated from under my very nose.

"And it was with a deep sigh that, as I launched one of several paper airplanes within easy reach, I began to ponder greener pastures. Either that or start all over...

"The next day I walked into class and said, "How would you like to start a magazine? And that's how Foxfire began."

When I walked into his class six years later, Foxfire was a nationally known folklore magazine with subscriptions in all fifty states and a dozen foreign countries; and *"The Foxfire Book,"* a collection of articles from the magazine, had just been published.

Wise Solomon said, "Where there is no vision, the people perish..." Wig's vision was outside the classroom. In his farsighted gaze, I discerned a royal kinship with the mountains. After connecting with us, he arose from his student desk. Pointing out a window that framed mountain peaks, basking in blue heavenly haze, he said, "Our text books are not in here, but out there. Your grandparents are leaving our lives daily. When they are gone so are magnificent hunting tales, ghost stories, tricks of self-sufficiency, suffering and sharing and building and healing, planting by the signs of the moon, plus so much more. This information will be lost forever if we do not collect and save it now."

Perhaps that was the spark that started the glow of Foxfire within. Or, perhaps Foxfire filled a deep void left inside me since Granny Lou's passing. Perhaps both. His words empowered my strongest sentiments and interest, mountain culture. Foxfire became a needful addiction with the inability to break away from its purpose. The name "Foxfire" was chosen by Wig's original class in 1966. It is taken from a bioluminescent fungi (Foxfire), growing on decaying wood in the Appalachian Mountains. The organism sheds a magnificent glow in the dark. It is a divine gift, shining the way on dark paths for weary travelers and straying students like me. The stunning colors are blue and green. Blue represents royalty. Green is symbolic of God himself. The great book of Hosea says, "I am like a green fir tree. From me thy fruit is found...."

The Foxfire class was a combination of many subjects: English, history, geography, science, writing, typing, editing, layout, and photography. Hands-on learning included developing and printing photographs, equipment repair, bookkeeping, filing, marketing, circulation, banking, public speaking, public relations, environmental issues, and much more. Wig had found the answer to student boredom and restlessness.

Collections of articles from Foxfire Magazine were published by Doubleday in *"The Foxfire Book"* in 1972. It astonished all of us by becoming an immediate best seller. Wig wrote in the introduction, "If this book is worth anything at all, it's because every piece of it was put together and handled and squeezed and shaped and touched by teenagers. And it's been a long time since I found a paper airplane under my desk."

Over the years a series of books followed in

sequence through Foxfire 12. Many specialty books added to Foxfire's glow: *"Memories of a Mountain Shortline," "Aunt Arie: A Foxfire Portrait," "The Foxfire Book of Appalachian Cookery," "A Foxfire Christmas,"* to list a few.

Foxfire was well staffed with dedicated personnel. The first adult staff member to appear on the scene was Suzy Angier. She had originally come to the mountains from Woodbridge, Connecticut, as a VISTA volunteer. Wig referred to her as his salvation. She lifted much weight from his overloaded wagon. I recall her love for the mountains, and her personal way of bonding with Foxfire contacts and students. Bright eyes and huge smiles brought Connecticut warmth to the south. "Suzy" means lily. She bloomed where she was planted in God's rich pasture.

Rabun native and Rabun Gap-Nacoochee School graduate Patrick Rogers returned to the county with a degree from the University of Georgia in journalism. He joined the Foxfire staff and took over responsibility of our school newspaper, "The Talon." Pat was like a cowboy with a rope, tying articles and activity together. He worked tirelessly, involving more students in Foxfire's purpose. Pat has the gift of humor. Laughter is the best medicine. Foxfire contact, Aunt Arie Carpenter, said, "I don't reckon th' devil'll get me fer laughin', but if he does, he'll shore get me 'cause I've always done more 'n' my share a th' laughin' in the world."

Margie Bennett was the glue of Foxfire operations. She joined the staff in my junior year. She was a "by the book" mentor who said what she meant and meant what she said. A sure fire way to make a' body mad is to tell them the truth. She did not hold back, as she told me her deep unmovable convictions about education, challenging my decision to quit school. That irritated me at the time. "Margie" means a pearl. Pearls are formed by tiny irritating grains of sand inside a hard shell. Oysters are wonderful examples in forming pearls. They add layers of protection to ease the irritation, resulting in natural gems. Margie believed each student was a pearl and worked to layer us with plenty of responsibility and accountability. She worked on cracking my hard, self-centered shell. When she was not fulfilling her duty in front of an IBM typewriter or poring over mounds of pieced together articles, she was out in the field with kids and recorders.

Wig and his staff called forth eagle spirits inside unincorporated kids who had been perched on dead limbs too long. Eagles are symbolic of a special class of people whose vision is above barnyards. Eagles mate for life. Years later, we remain lifted by the power we saw, heard, smelled, tasted, and touched.

One prime example of the secret of the mountains was our beloved contact, Aunt Arie Carpenter.

From Wig's book, "Moments," he writes: "Aunt Arie Carpenter is one of a number of contacts with whom we keep in touch who has that power. A visit to her log house is a sure-fire fine experience every time, for each time she insists on feeding the kids who come and gets them all to help her cook the meal on her ancient, wood-burning stove.

"Once when we visited, she was trying to get the eyeballs out of a hog's head so that she could make souse meat. She couldn't do it alone, and so she got the kid I had taken, Paul Gillespie, to help her. The record of that interview forms one of the early chapters in *"The Foxfire Book."*

Aunt Arie. (Photo used with permission of The Foxfire Museum and Heritage Center, Mountain City, GA)

"The moment I always savor," says Wig,
"Whenever I take kids up to her log house—and
I've done it hundreds of times—is when it's time to
leave. Without fail and without prior instruction,
it's just natural and spontaneous every time, the
kids line up to say goodbye to her individually.
She always grasps the hand of each, looks into
each face for a long time and says, "You be sure to
come back now. I'll be thinking about you while
you're gone. Don't forget me." And as we walk over
the hill, we look back at her standing on the porch
watching us go, and she often says as she waves,
"Now's when I'll be lonely..."

Wig was the son she never had. When we visited without him, she asked, "Where is Eliot? He is
always on th' go. I miss him; y'all take care of
Eliot." Then she arose from a wooden chair seated
near the fireplace to hug and pound us in the
back and plant moist affectionate kisses on each
young cheek. The Foxfire gang became grandchildren in a quiver from God. Aunt Arie embraced
everyone, the very picture of love.

LIVE MEAT

Foxfire's staff soared above molting kids, dropping live meat like eagles on mountaintops caring for their own. Margie persistently dropped unfinished articles on us for completion. Hands-on experience is live meat. I took materials home for a beginner's taste. Dad roosted with the chickens; lights went out after dark. I sat crosslegged in front of a dying fire surrounded by mounds of cassette tapes, papers, pictures, scissors, contact cement, and a dictionary. I changed positions regularly to catch reflections flickering off the plank ceiling. It was enough light to work.

Resting occasionally, I gazed into the glowing flames, thinking about tomorrow's journey and studying slow-burning logs in the consuming fire. The thick bark melted away first, then the very core turned into ashes. The logs changed form. Ashes are still wood. I saw a picture of myself being changed within. The glowing encouragement of Foxfire's staff changed my educational direction, and they became a caring second family.

Every involved student was caught up in the glow of achievement. Foxfire students became glowing lanterns with legs. Armed with faith, tape recorders, and cameras, we captured mountain secrets, sounding our heritage like trumpets that eventually resonated across the nation. To date the books have sold over nine million copies and still going. A miracle indeed. Wig said, "Life just isn't worth living until you bet all you've got on something you believe in."

I believed in Foxfire's purpose and became absorbed in a personality article about Maude Shope, a fiercely independent, seventy-six-year-old woman who still rode her mule, Frank.

"I never did try t' drive a car. My mule is th' way I got around. I've had him since he was eighteen months old. He'll be thirty-two in February. You can drag wood with him—anything y' want t' do. Yes, sir, he's something."

I wanted to meet Miss Maude, so fellow student Sheila Vinson and I went with Margie on our first interview. It was late fall when autumn hues were all but gone, exposing bare mountains stretching fold on fold. The evening sun was hidden by thick black clouds threatening rain. A doozy of a storm loomed in the still mountain air. Jagged lightning bolts streaked the sky. It looked like the whole earth was blowing up. Loud thunder jarred the ground slightly, shaking Margie's green Suburban. Heavy rain pelted down like a cow peein' on a flat rock. I thought of the fountains of the deep, bustin' open in the Bible. Fallen limbs cluttered the roadside and draped rusty barbed-wire fence lines. Margie pulled off the road until the rain slowed; then we went on up a path with knee high ditches gutted by the rain.

A host of loud, barking dogs announced our arrival. Wet chickens scurried in the yard, then huddled together like people smothering themselves in close company. I was glad not to be in the classroom. Miss Maude appeared in the doorway of a tiny abode. She wore an old sweater pulled over a patterned dress and apron. A tight-fitting toboggan topped her head. Her eyes revealed wisdom and self-sufficiency. "That storm was like th' devil a-beatin' tan bark, Come on in before ye drown. I look like the hind wheels on bad luck, but I ain't lookin' fer no feller." Callused hands showed much work and held a cattle prod. Thin tubs and feed buckets lined the front of the house.

"You take stock and them blamed old dogs—well, they're company t' a body. A dog usually comes ahead of anything else, don't it? You know yourself that you'll hold up for your dog. If somebody was t' come in and kick that dog just t' get t' kick him, I'd fly all mad in spite of myself, I guess."

We covered many subjects as the recorder ran. As we paused to change tapes, Miss Maude continued: "I'll tell you what I'm afraid of. You may live t' see it; I won't. There is s' many more people being born that have to have a place to live. We've got land here. In a few years they'll cut it up and they'll take off so much and sell it. That worries me. There's so many new houses put up down th' road in just th' last little while. I wouldn't swap this little shack for the finest house in New York. I wouldn't do it. That's just th' way I feel."

Before we left, she amazed us by riding her mule through the pasture. Soon after that interview, we were saddened to hear Maude died. She never saw her worry come to pass. That article jump-started me onto other articles Margie was happy to find.

As interest in Foxfire expanded far beyond Rabun County, so did national invitations to travel

Maude and Frank. (Photo used with permission of The Foxfire Museum and Heritage Center, Mountain City, GA)

and share the glow. It was rare for me to go beyond County lines. The first trip Wig took me on was with fellow students Dana Williams and Claude Rickman to Washington D.C. We loaded inside his white long wheelbase Ford pickup truck en route to the Atlanta airport. I watched out the rear window as mountains faded from view, somewhat nervous about leaving and not knowing what to expect at an airport. I had never seen an airplane apart from those flying high over our home. As a small child, Mama told us stories about Uncle Millard "driving" airplanes in the Air Force. When we heard approaching sounds, Ernest and I dropped our play to chase the plane through the pasture, arms raised waving frantically until the plane left sight. We hoped it was Uncle Millard and that he heard our yells, "Throw down some candy, bubble gum and toys." One day while prowling through the deep woods we stumbled upon a box of discarded toys and red phonograph records. Fading Bazooka bubble gum papers convinced us Uncle Millard had made a drop.

As we approached Atlanta I counted hundreds of transfer trucks heading north and wondered how the mountains would be affected if suddenly the supply route was stopped.

Wig pulled into the airport parking lot and stopped. He said, "Lock the doors," a practice almost unheard of in the mountains. Shoving his keys deep into jean pockets he said, "This is it."

I was amazed at the actual size of a Delta jet moving up and down landing strips. My first ride on an escalator brought us to the ticket counter. Boarding for our flight was called out and we were off into the wild blue yonder. Wig insisted I sit by the window. Once in the air lightning danced on the silver wings through a big storm. The pilot said the plane was hitting air pockets and the reason for gentle bumps in the air. A uniformed stewardess served my first-ever turkey sandwich with yellow mustard. It was pretty good. I was unsure how Wig was going to get us from Washington's big airport to our mission, but trusted he might know what he was doing. He got us to our hotel rooms located high above the ground floor, overlooking the city. Dana and I were helped up the elevator by a bellhop who lingered in our room for a bit, then sorta slammed the door when leaving. His action was rude by mountain ways.

We asked Wig, "What was his problem?" Wig asked, "Did you tip him?" I said, "What did he need advice about?"

Finally we reached our mission, to spread the glow of Foxfire. Standing before a packed audience of total strangers at the Washington Hilton with unrehearsed speeches was easy because Wig believed in us. He knew we could do it. The only thing strange was the luxurious thick carpet under mountain feet and the newspaper Wig was reading in the afternoon after we finished. He pointed to a picture of a salmon-colored Mustang involved in a robbery. It was shot to pieces, totally ruining a nice car, just a block away from our hotel.

Before leaving Washington D.C., Wig treated us to a trip to one of the biggest museums in the world, The Smithsonian Institute. I was breathless standing beside literal historic documents. Betsy Ross's first American flag, real dinosaur skeletons, moon rocks and the Hope diamond were mind-blowing experiences. It was displayed near Appalachia's own gem collections. I remain addicted to museums and dream of another visit to the mighty Smithsonian. We packed in all we could on our short trip including The Washington Monument and the Lincoln Memorial. Foxfire afforded kids like me priceless experiences outside our own culture.

When I arrived back home, Dad became suspicious of my all-consuming fascination with Foxfire.

The more he thought about it, the more apprehensive he became, forbidding me to go to New York and appear on the "Today Show." It did no good to argue with my fascination so he just said, "You ain't going. I saw on television they kill people up there. You flat ain't going." Mama's intervention did no good. "I don't see how he keeps a hat on such a narrow mind." She used covert activity for my second trip; to Berkeley, California. I was packed and gone south towards the Atlanta airport before Dad came home from work.

Mama joked, "I'll keep an ear and eye open towards the sky. If yellow stuff falls, messin' up the windows, I'll know you did it." The windows remained clean because we flew south over Florida making the first stop in Dallas, Texas.

Our plane flew over the beautiful Golden Gate Bridge that connected San Francisco with Berkeley. We stayed with the Brown family while on mission to help a school establish a similar Foxfire program. They were happy to show us around town. I marveled at San Francisco's steep streets traveled by trolley cars and at ships moving in the bay.

Lots of walking gave us an appetite. Wig took us to a Japanese restaurant. They were stingy with their soup. The thimble size bowl was clear like water. I didn't know whether to spoon it or drink it. Bean sprouts were a first for me because in the mountains, we eat the other part of beans.

The cook began to juggle sharp knives into the air as he worked mutilating pieces of chicken right on the eating table in front of us. When he got finished, you couldn't tell it was chicken. (It wasn't southern fried.) I recalled Dad's words, "Don't eat nothing you wasn't raised on; you will get sick." California-style food was a shocker for this Georgia mountain native. Wig saved my life with a bucket of Kentucky Fried Chicken.

The next day we visited Fisherman's Wharf and a park that buzzed with activity, full of strange people passing out flowers and selling peace signs. Since I messed up in Washington, D.C. by not giving money to the bellhop, I decided to help California out and bought a stained glass peace sign. Dad would not allow it hung in our house saying it looked like a broken cross. This trip was much longer so I was glad to come home. Wig stopped his pickup truck for gasoline just before the Rabun County line. I got out and kissed Mother Earth.

My life returned to normal. "Normal" included my failing senior English, which was taught by a former college professor. I had little interest in Pygmalion. She had little interest in my fascination with Foxfire. Wig's teaching methods greatly differed from traditional classrooms and teachers. My constant absence from English class to work on Foxfire projects was one reason I was failing. Naturally, she grew agitated because she felt rightfully responsible for our academic future.

I was totally absorbed in writing an article for Seventeen Magazine. One day the professor curiously approached my desk to investigate papers I fiddled with. Among pink and yellow form papers was a letter from their editor.

SEVENTEEN
320 Park Avenue
New York, NY 10022

Dear Barbara,
Enclosed are the rights agreement forms for your article "The Greening of Foxfire"... As soon as I receive the signed forms, I can process payment. You should receive a check for $400 about three weeks later...

Sincerely,
Eleanor Fairclough

The professor was shocked, delighted, and very supportive.

The cafeteria cashier was shocked when I paid for a six-cent carton of milk with a one hundred dollar bill.

My family was shocked and humbled when a new bedroom suite arrived.

I was shocked by stacks of fan mail and increases in Foxfire subscriptions.

Mama jested, "Great day in th' morning! If this keeps up we'll all have to wear a shock absorber around our neck."

Reviews followed: "Barbara Taylor, June graduate of Rabun Gap-Nacoochee School and veteran Foxfire staff member, has described her experience working on the magazine in the September issue of Seventeen. The article is entitled, 'The Greening of Foxfire.' It's dynamite." (Institute for Development of Educational Activities, Washington, D.C.)

The most significant part of that review in 1973 is, "June graduate of Rabun Gap-Nacoochee School."

My dreaded sentence had ended in liberating triumph.

I now found I was heading into two more life-changing experiences.

PART II

WHEELS OF CHANGE

TYING KNOTS

In the fall of 1972, Dad was using a mule-drawn plough smoothing up a new yard surrounding a new home located just above our old one.

A blueprint of his dream was kept inside a

Dad and the mule

small homemade wooden box with a lock. Each payday he made small cash deposits into a worn envelope tucked beside family pictures, a half gallon jar of moonshine, land deeds and a huge roll of cash register sale receipts. "If your Mama ever tucks tail and leaves she can never swear I did not feed her." Mama replied, "And you can't swear I didn't cook and feed you!"

Beside the new house lay a pile of large oak logs snaked from the mountain with mules. He sought a skilled sawyer for those oak logs waiting to become porch lumber. Someone recommended William Woodall and his son Larry.

Soon after, a slim, shy young man came to our house driving a huge log truck. He opened a squeaking door on the truck, got out and fiddled with attaching steel cables to the heavy timber. He was the sawyer's son, working after school with his dad. My dad jested, "That boy learned to run the chain saw in the Sahara Forest; it's a desert now."

When Larry returned to deliver Dad's lumber, we became acquainted. He joined my close knit Foxfire friends, Mary Thomas and Laurie Brunson and became an ever-present support. Before I was legally licensed to drive, Larry came each Friday night to take Mary and me to school basketball games. Sometimes we all hung out at the Dairy Queen watching young people "drag town" or hung out at Laurie's house. No matter what activity we chose, Larry and I gravitated to the company of my closest friends.

In the summer of 1972, I was hired to work in the Foxfire office. Wig gave me a salary advance

that bought my first car, a 1965 red Ford
Fairlane, named the "Red Demon." He said we
should paint yellow and orange flames behind the
rear tires. Larry, Mary, and I bought a cheap bot-
tle of Boone's Farm strawberry wine. We all piled
into the slick-shined front seat with intentions of
a proper celebration. Fifteen minutes later, Larry
crashed us into another car that had made an illegal U-turn in the road. Mary's head was harder
than the windshield that shattered. When the car
stopped spinning, Larry tore his buttoned shirt off
to mop the red juice off Mary's face. After I
retrieved my eyeglasses wrapped around a window
knob, I searched the ditch lines for my shiny hub-
caps. First on the scene was a woman driving a
pickup truck. She reached inside the "Red
Demon', grabbed our wine and threw it over the
bank before the cops and ambulance arrived. We
went with Mary to the hospital. The doctor picked
fragments of glass from her forehead and wrapped
it up. We felt so bad and couldn't leave her side.
Our souls were knit together. Laurie, Mary, Larry,
and I had all things common.

On March 2, 1974, we all four paused our
busy schedules for Larry and me to "get hitched."
Larry and I asked Dad to come but he said, "I'd as
soon go to a funeral." I guess he dreaded the loss
of a daughter. We borrowed the closest preacher
from Rabun Gap-Nacoochee and gathered at the
home of Foxfire mentors Bob and Margie Bennett
who, at that time, lived on the RGNS school campus. Bob laughed as he told Larry, "You know you
are marrying three today; you better RUN!"

The blue jean wedding was short and sweet.

Both our cars were decked out with tin cans tied to the exhaust, balloons, tissue and the worst: canned sardines poured on top of the motors. After we regained consciousness from the severe pelting of rice, Larry and I escaped in his car. Laurie and Mary took my car into town to clean it. Spectators strained their eyes and fogged their bifocals at the sight of two women in a "newlywed car." It was hilarious. Mama said, "If that is not the mark of true friends, there ain't a cow in Texas."

Larry parked his stump jumper and hung up his chainsaw when we moved to Kelly's Creek on Dad's property. He began working at Rabun Quarries. The employees changed his name from Larry to DOO because he sang happy songs like:

*"Camp town ladies sing this song
Doo-dah Doo-dah
Camp town racetrack five miles long
O Doo-dah day"*

In keeping with long-time tradition at the quarry, all DOO's co-workers have funny nicknames. Pappy, Jaybird, Mossy Jaws, Sweetie, Dibble-Dabble, Daddy Rabbit, and Chigger are a few. I probably would not recognize their real names in conversation.

DOO is a man of few words, probably because he can't get a word in edgewise around home. Once he asked me if I needed ice packs for my jaws. (He limped for a while, but recovered okay.)

Larry and I were twenty-four years old when

our daughter, Melissa, was born October 4, 1978.

Mary's mother, Mrs. Thomas, called every day to check on us during the pregnancy. She said, "Barbara, the old-fashion nurses prepare the maternity ward on full moons. October 4th the moon will be full. If you don't go into labor then, you will probably wait until the next full moon." She was right.

There was no such thing as an epidural at Rabun County Hospital back then. Somewhere in their junk pile is a pair of stainless steel bed rails twisted like hair pins.

After Larry, Melissa, and I came home, Wig dropped by with a yellow baby quilt he had asked Foxfire contact Ada Kelly to make. Melissa still treasures his gift today.

Parenting was a wonderful opportunity to experience miracles as we watched new lives unfold. We witnessed the young belonging to the mountains. I recall the first time small feet touched fresh cut grass to follow lazy grasshoppers through the yard and their first quest to hold a butterfly by its winking yellow wings. God allows us precious times to see through the eyes of a child and experience unconditional love.

Our son Isaac (means laughter) was born ten years later, January 28, 1988. Thank God for epidurals by then! He had red hair and a temper.

Some common sayings here in bad economic times are: "Granny boiled the dishrag to make soup." "We eat cereal with a fork to save the milk for coffee." "The dog leaves home each night at supper time." And the great parental favorite, "We are just gonna have t' make do." DOO said, "Ain't nobody making DOO do nothing!"

I ain't no preacher, but a friend once asked me to speak at her wedding. DOO and I have attended two weddings, and we would have sent somebody else to our own if we could have. A search for a white jacket for me to wear landed us with a sales lady. She asked, "How about a bright blouse with this jacket?" I said, "It has got to be white." "Oooh," said the sales lady, "It's a black and white wedding." DOO was swift to hear and slow to speak. Finally he said, "Why, no, nice lady, they are both white folks, born that way."

DOO and I argue just to keep warm. A recent loud reasoning happened when we prepared our living wills. DOO expressed strongly his detesting of life support hookups. I had his big screen HD television disconnected. (It's back on now; nuff said!)

He must watch "rasslin" twice a week. It is the only sport in the world where the fans know more than the referees. We can smell onions on sweating men, holding each other on the big screen. DOO knows it's fake, but he likes it better than cartoons.

He is not too keen on other sports. One fall DOO and I took his mother, Clara, through Clemson, South Carolina, during the Tiger football season. Miles upon miles of bumper-to-bumper traffic lined the roads. The orange team flags on each vehicle resembled hometown funeral alert flags. The long procession caused my mother-in-law to remark, "This fellow must have been well-liked; look at all these cars trying to get to the funeral!"

DOO and I enjoy spending time in the mountains with our grandson, Sterling. He is ten years old and has a healthy respect for preserving nature.

We believe the best things parents can give children, besides Christ, are an education and then a house. DOO and I have built four simple houses and pray our children will hold on to them. The latest was built from salvage when during heavy rain, a resort house slid off the mountain above our property. We got permission to take the materials. Our son, Isaac, 22, now enjoys a nice two-story house, debt-free.

Two fine jersey cows watched us measure, saw, and dodge mad hammers. They never "uddered" a sound, but later they went back and ate the pink insulation from underneath the house. DOO said, "I sure hope they don't get sick. On the brighter side, when they 'freshin,' (give birth) the calves will be warm with little pink sweaters. Let's put sunglasses on the cows. When it snows we can save on hay."

DOO and I will soon celebrate thirty-eight years together. That seems like a long time to look across a bowl of gravy at the same face. A good mate is the best gift God will ever give us, except Christ.

DOO

PEOPLE OF GRANITE

Rabun Quarries is our county's oldest surviving industry. Founded in the 1940s by our neighbors, Claude and Bea Kelly, it has been a part of life here for three generations. Mr. Kelly's business eye saw a need for crushed stone. He put to use his inheritance, a fascinating solid granite mountain. The quarry produced highly prized stones for construction. Granite is a very hard and durable rock, akin to the Kelly character. When local people think of Kelly's Creek his giant solid granite mountain comes to mind.

Aunt Oshie and her family lived about a mile from our house and within a stone's cast away from quarry operations in a ten-dollar-a-month rented house. She was the first-born of my beloved Granny Lou and Grandpa Taylor. A look into her face triggered fond memories still fresh since Granny Lou's passing. I suppose her unusual name came from the Bible (Numbers 13:8). "Oshie" was the only word Granny Lou could proudly spell.

When I was young, Dad would let me stay with Aunt Oshie while he went to town. Hopping from the back of his pickup truck, I made my way up a steep path lined with huge oak trees towards an old house supported by stilts. I stopped to watch Dad steer past giant granite boulders that lined the main road, passing through the quarry. Vehicles, including the school bus, passed underneath a moving conveyer belt carrying stones for processing.

Grandpa Ale Taylor, Granny Lou and baby Oshie

Aunt Oshie and Uncle Albert sat on an uneven, decaying porch surrounded by large cardboard boxes filled with scrap carpeting for recycling from the carpet mill. The rhythm of hands working at stringing rugs was accompanied by daily devouring sounds filtering from the quarry. Jackhammer steel with diamond-tipped drill bits pounded holes in hard granite like monster woodpeckers. Mighty wheels squeaked, turning the jaw crusher. Aunt Oshie commented, "If a man fell into the crusher, he'd turn into sausage on the conveyer belt." Bulldozers and trucks ran constantly up and down the steep granite road. August heat vapors emerged on the stone-faced mountain like demons rising from the pit.

My brother, Ellis, loaded dynamite into granite

The Quarry

holes, preparing for the next day's blast. In the afternoons Mama placed cool towels over his watery eyes to ease dynamite headaches from nitrogen exposure.

Our community grew accustomed to blasting. A sure sign to take cover was an eerie stillness hanging in the air like Halloween. Traffic was blocked on Kelly's Creek road. Workmen on the mountain took cover underneath heavy equipment. Other employees made their way to a small metal shop to wait. Aunt Oshie went nowhere.

The eerie stillness lingered before the earth trembled deep within. Low rumbling vibrations felt like a million soldiers marching underground just before the grand finale.

We watched large gray boulders like elephants on springboards rise into the sky, then crash back onto the earth. Aunt Oshie kept a careful eye on the path of smaller stones sailing through the air like arrows dipped in fire. Showers of stone snapped tree branches, crashing near her house. Shreds of green leaves drifted through the air and into the yard. She said it would be like that when

Gabriel blew the trumpet. I hoped not.

Another thick cloud of gray dust added layers to everything around and inside the house. When the wind blew, grains of sand sounded like pelting sleet on the windowpanes.

Eventually, she moved several miles away from the quarry. Her final days were spent in a singlewide trailer near a son. Battles for breath made restful sleep impossible. Her bedside aids were an oxygen tank and a wooden ironing board that held a weary head through long nights of thin air.

Did years of exposure to granite dust cause her condition? No one knows, but it's a hell of a way to end your days—on an ironing board, gasping for breath.

I am sure the founders of Rabun Quarries had no knowledge of the dangers of granite dust; neither could they dictate where neighbors lived. In fact, Mr. Kelly and his family worked in the industry and lived at the entrance of operations.

About 1973, the year I graduated from Rabun Gap-Nacoochee, Mr. Kelly leased the family business. Rabun Quarry eventually became Vulcan Materials, a giant corporation. Big changes began to occur. Modern equipment was installed to meet production demands. Other businesses dependent on quarry products moved to Kelly's Creek to be closer to resources.

Two asphalt plants and a concrete operation became our new neighbors. Tall pipes pumped black smoke in the air choking mountain views, surrounding homes with tainted haloes. House ventilation filters became loaded with soot.

Natural fog kept the smoke trapped for hours until it lifted. The smell of hot tar and diesel caused headaches and irritated eyes, keeping some residents housebound until the shank of the day (11:00 AM).

The community tolerated added traffic, noise and pollution longer than we should before say-

Smoke from the old Asphalt Plant

ing, "ENOUGH!" A meeting was arranged with industry officials and county commissioners in a rented room. We feared more heavy industry was coming. Tension was stronger than the coffee they provided. Safety concerns were voiced. One commissioner stormed, "WHERE were you people when this property was zoned heavy industrial?" An elderly neighbor arose with the help of a cane and said, "Fightin' a war." A woman asked, "If silica dust is hazardous, why has the community never been advised?"

On the back of gravel invoices is this warning: "HEALTH HAZARD WARNING: THIS PRODUCT CONTAINS CRYSTALLINE SILICA. WARNING: AVOID BREATHING EXCESSIVE DUST *Breathing silica-containing dust for prolonged periods in the workplace can cause lung damage and a lung disease called silicosis. *Several scientific organizations have classified crystalline silica as causing lung cancer in humans. "Silicosis or lung cancer can result in permanent injury or death. Read the Material Safety Data Sheet (MSDS) before handling this product to determine the appropriate ventilation or respiratory protection necessary to safeguard your health. The risk of silicosis or lung cancer depends upon the duration and levels of silica exposure."

I asked, "Does anyone think it unusual that over twenty residents within a mile radius of operations have died from cancer over a period of years?" Officials deemed this as normal statistics. Apparently, distance from the dust is a plus factor.

Vulcan Material's environmental representative took our concerns seriously. He said as soon as one asphalt plant finished their current contract, they would be history. The one remaining had its equipment on the ground for repair shortly after the meeting. It was eventually replaced by an entirely new plant.

Currently there are ten commercial businesses making tracks on our short road. Huge rubber tires whine constantly, exporting and importing products. Loaded gravel and concrete trucks can weigh thirty-five tons, taking all the road they want. Nobody has ever walked away from a wreck on Kelly's Creek.

We asked a team of three county commissioners to widen our narrow road, reduce the speed limit and erect flashing lights at school bus stops in blind curves—three reasons Kelly's Creek road is more dangerous than any other county road. The community got empty promises. Commissioner Bobby Welch agreed with our concerns. The other two seemed hard of hearing. Our dangerous road remains unaided. One elected official remarked, "Kelly's Creek road is no more dangerous than other roads in the county."

A New Direction: Marbarla

My zeal for Foxfire continued after my graduation. Wig encouraged us on new paths beyond the classroom. He desired graduates to walk out the doors and become involved in issues affecting our changing community and culture.

Foxfire had not developed social and environmental involvement except for a brochure alerting mountain visitors to the mindless pillage of wild flowers. With the help of grant money, Foxfire was able to launch our own social and environmental team. I, along with two fellow students, Mary Thomas and Laurie Brunson, were hired for a full year to look at issues affecting mountain culture. The project's name, MARBARLA was taken from our names: MARy, BARbara, and LAurie.

Our then Governor, Jimmy Carter, encouraged moviemakers to use Georgia; some did exactly that. Hollywood filmmakers traveled three thousand miles to the North Georgia Mountains, looking for depraved hillbillies. They came with dollars and cameras in one hand, a copy of James Dickey's novel, "Deliverance", in the other.

Their cameras rolled right here in our county and the surrounding area, capturing the fictional adventure of four city slickers who come to the mountains looking to prove their manhood on the wild and scenic Chattooga River only to run head long into hillbilly hell. The damnable stereotyping of Appalachian people and repulsive, graphic scenes would make any viewer leery to venture onto mountain paths.

After reading only a few descriptive words about our beloved people from Dickey's book, we were outraged and breathing fire. Wig used quotes from Dell's paperback. "The sort of men you mock, but at the same time are relieved to be rid of (pg.64). The sort of men that are 'creatures' (58) from whom you expect nothing but mean words and know if you see them in the woods are tending their still (44). The sort of men who jump like dogs on their hind legs (54), or who are 'albino' or splay-eyed or 'demented' or worse (54-55)."

The "worse" was a homosexual rape scene filmed on the river, showing movie star, Ned Beatty, being abused by wild hillbillies. The scene was beyond smoke in Foxfire's nose.

No other identifiable regional, cultural people group in America would sit idly by without protesting such deadly wounds and vile insults inflicted on their character and integrity. The very people represented by Foxfire magazine and the Foxfire books had been assaulted before America on the silver screen by Hollywood money mongrels who could care less.

The MARBARLA team was given its first assignment: investigate the impact of the Deliverance movie on the very place where it was filmed, our own community. Emotional reaction was one of our greatest challenges—we had to be careful not to influence our contacts, but let them speak their mind. Over a three-month period Mary, Laurie and I collected information from local people, county officials and rescue workers regarding repercussions of the Deliverance movie experienced in our area.

About half a dozen local people were enlisted to play small, demeaning roles. They were used like menstrual cloths, paid some money and tossed. Most of the people we talked to did not have a clue what was done to them as Hollywood pointed cameras and sucked out souls.

A disturbing scene was shot at the home of a chief Foxfire contact, Mrs. Webb. She sat beside a hopelessly deformed child. "They come here and they wanted me and the baby in the movie." That child was her granddaughter, paralyzed at birth. Mrs. Webb never left her side. "There sets a baby I've brought through so far with prayers. She's going on fourteen years old, and I have to feed her. I have to give her a bath. I have to tend to her the same as if she was six months old. And it's getting hard on me. She stayed in the hospital out yonder for three or four months. They never did do any good. Well, what the Lord does is done right." Mrs. Webb's deep compassion and commitment was ignored as moviemakers portrayed her and her granddaughter in images that suggested they were mountain freaks.

The movie crew altered Mrs. Webb's property for filming. "I had that little patch down there planted with 'taters (potatoes). They was just a- coming up, and they wanted to put a road through there, and they plowed them up. Yes, they paid me for them, but not what they ought to. You know a patch of 'taters like that is worth something. The 'taters were awful pretty, but I didn't grumble. I ain't too long here and, when I leave here, I want to go in peace. Craving money—I don't do that."

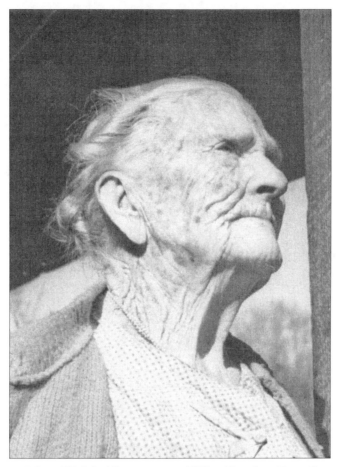

Mrs. Webb (Courtesy of The Foxfire Fund)

The famous dueling banjo scene was also filmed at Mrs. Webb's. Billy Redden was not chosen because of talent. Frank Rickman, local recruiter for the Hollywood film crew said, "Billy couldn't play it—chord it—you know. They put a trick shirt on Billy Redden." It was actually a pantomime.

Nell Norton, known as "Whispering Nell" because she was a very vocal gal, appeared in a dining room scene. "They didn't tell me what the movie was about. They said they'd like to take my picture. They said they would like to have me in the movie. They didn't tell me nothing."

Local man, Ronnie Deal, played a hired driver from Mrs. Webb's place.

"I didn't like them filming that little girl, but I couldn't have said too much to them to make them change their mind. I guess out of that week (working with the crew) that will be one thing I'll always remember."

Local resident Ed Ramey played a gas station attendant. "I think it ought to be a violation of the law to show pictures like that in the act. Them people stripped off down yonder on the river..." Ed knew nothing of the rape scene until his first viewing of the movie at a theater.

Part of our hands-on research was a raft trip down the now famous, "Deliverance" river, the Chattooga, with expeditionist Payson Kennedy of the Nantahala Outdoor Center. Payson worked as a stunt man with the movie crew.

My childhood on the calm banks of Kelly's Creek was no preparation for the wide, rushing, churning whitewater howling with a daring voice over great water-torn rocks. We were geared with helmets, life jackets, oars and prayer. Being in experienced company somewhat soothed my nervousness.

The river was stunningly beautiful, but we were shocked by the sight of piles of beer cans, old campfires, and fading Kleenex boxes that littered its banks. Droves of canoeists, rafters, spectators and curious moviegoers were coming out weekly to see "the Deliverance river" and leaving trash like a calling card.

From our raft, we recognized spots where scenes were filmed. Payson's daughter, Kathy, told us that many rafters fear mountain people who are fishing from the banks of the river. "I get pretty tired of people asking about Deliverance. Some of the rafters I have brought down here start squealing like pigs when we reach the part of the river where the rape scene was filmed. I don't care for that."

We recalled an interview with Mrs. Denton who lived near the river. "When river rats see me, they paddle quickly away looking back over their shoulder like I have supernatural powers to overtake and hurt them."

As rushing waters moved our raft swiftly downstream, my arms became very tired from using the guiding oars around and between large rocks. Sometimes a strong current threw us towards the banks. Fighting the river is one of the hardest challenges I've encountered even with four other people paddling hard. It isn't for sissies.

As we neared Woodall Shoals, probably the most dangerous spot in the river, the raft was pulled ashore. Looking into the raging water with enormous rocks at the bottom of the falls caused me to be thankful I could walk around this spot. Inexperienced tourists and thrill-seekers were no match for dangerous waters. Many had lost their lives, some right here, since the movie had been released. I suspected those who died here were probably very tired also, yet continued on without rest. I recalled Sheriff Chester York's advice, "Don't go down that river."

Chief Lindsey Moore, head of the Rabun County Rescue squad, lamented those he dragged from the raging waters. "They hear about it (the river) and they want to come try it to see what kind of a thrill they get out of it. They don't realize what danger they're getting into.

"Now lots of them just come down there and camp on the river and don't float it. Most every camping area you go to has garbage all over it everywhere. It's awful littered up, It used to be that I could go down that river and catch me a mess of fish most anytime I wanted. But now, it's littered up-the banks are slick; beer cans, garbage and what-have-you scattered all over and in the river."

James Dickey, author of the book and the man who wrote the movie script, tried to warn people: "That river doesn't care about you. It'll knock your brains out. Most of the people going up there don't know about whitewater rivers. They are just out for a lark, just like those characters in "Deliverance." They wouldn't have gone up there if I hadn't written the book. There's nothing I can do about it. I can't patrol the river. But it just makes me feel awful."

Rabun County Sheriff Chester York told us: "I think most of the accidents on the river are negligence and drinking, because we found out from the bodies that have been recovered, there's only been one that hadn't been drinking as I recall.

"I have been there helping to recover bodies.

The last body I helped recover was down north of the Highway 76 Bridge. When I arrived at the scene, it was probably five o'clock in the afternoon. There were at least twenty-five people passed before dark-canoes, rafts and so on-and there being a body there didn't affect them a bit. They didn't even stop and ask what had happened, even though there were some one hundred to one hundred fifty people there helping recover the body."

The Sheriff continued, "I've seen those rafts down there at Woodall Shoals on two occasions caught like flutter mills. There's hydraulic power in there. I've seen life jackets stripped off of the body (by the force of the water). You can tell people that and they still don't believe you. They have to find out the hard way. Quite a few of them do find out the hard way." (According to a report compiled by The United States Forest Service, nearly forty fatalities occurred between 1970-2003 on the mighty river.)

Our findings appeared in a sixteen-page report as a centerfold in the winter Foxfire Magazine of 1973. The title of our article was taken from an old Baptist hymnal, "He Shouted Loud, Hosanna, DELIVERANCE will come."

It has been nearly forty years since Hollywood's deadly invasion of our community. Occasionally, tee shirts and bumper stickers still appear: "If You Hear Banjos Paddle Faster!" The scar remains.

It is Thanksgiving Day as I finish this very piece. Darkness is falling like a curtain on a light-ed stage. The forest floor is thick and silent with blankets of protective brown leaves. Evening song-birds have gone. Kelly's Creek sings solo over the same spring rocks. A little while ago the stillness was shattered by our dog, Charlie. Looking up from my text, I saw him streak lightning-fast through the yard like Old Yeller after a bear. I ran outside to investigate the ruckus and glimpsed two lost young hikers and their dog disappearing up a mountain path. DOO went to see if he could help and brought them back here to our home. They were shaken, but grateful for our phone and water. As they waited to be picked up, the young woman said, "This was really scary; thank you for helping us. My friend and I were just talking about Deliverance country."

I asked, "Do you hear any pigs squealing?"

We wished the movie scars would vanish like the moviemakers who sharpened their cinematic knives and dealt us the wounds, but they don't. Mountain people are still feared and stared at by tourists from the safety of vehicles. Spectators peel their eyes, as they pass through, hoping to see a real-life-honest-to-God hillbilly hick straight from the land of nine-fingered people. We fight stereotyping with truth.

A big chunk of truth and antidote for Deliverance was the very successful Broadway play, *"Foxfire."* Hume Cronyn and co-writer Susan Cooper came to Georgia, wanting to purchase the dramatic rights to the Foxfire material from stu-dents and staff. Susan wrote about their experi-ence: " We both went to Georgia to explain to a group of stern-eyed youngsters that we were not out to frame their cherished old people in another version of Lil' Abner. They gave us the only two chairs in Wig's office and sat around us on the floor; we felt singularly nervous and about a hundred years old. When our pitch was made, we went out and paced the green, cricket-shirring hill while they deliberated; then a lad in jeans and boots came and whistled. 'Y'all can come back in now,' he said, sphinx-like; then he grinned, relenting, 'I guess we think you're okay.' That was one milestone: a rush of relief that told us how much we now wanted to translate the spirit of Foxfire into theater."

Sometime later Hallmark made the movie, "Foxfire", starring Jessica Tandy, Hume Cronyn, and John Denver. Both play and movie portrayed truth and helped dispel lies from the granddaddy of mountain horror flicks, *"Deliverance."*

MARBARLA's next assignment was a sobering one: to do a study on a local community in change. We chose as our representative area Betty's Creek: a beautiful, narrow, winding valley with rolling green pastures, stunning mountain views, flashing waters, the best trout fishing in the country, and people who were close-knit, caring and friendly. The creek itself in that valley had been named for a local midwife many years before.

We started out with our usual tape recorders, camera, and a list of questions. Before long the enormity of what we were tackling began to hit us. As we listened to elders of the community pass down the history of the settling of Betty's Creek, we accompanied them to old home places and

Betty's Creek

began to visually and emotionally absorb the living images they were imparting to us.

Growing up in this isolated community meant "If you didn't build it, raise it or make it, you didn't have it," and neighbors always stood ready to pitch in and help take up the slack. We located the tiny "Last Chance" one-room schoolhouse, the only school most of the older community members had ever attended. It was no longer occupied but still standing. We visited the old water-powered gristmill that had been restored by Mary Hambidge. It was operating, still taking a measure of corn as payment. As we talked to the miller Claude Darnell, watched farmers Grover Bradley and Jess Rickman bring in their sacks of home-grown corn, and smelled and tasted the fresh-ground meal, we were moved by a sense of time-lessness.

That sense did not last, however.

The generation we were listening to was the generation that had gone from riding in horse-drawn wagons and plowing with mules to seeing men on the moon. The Betty's Creek community had been so isolated by impassably rough, mud roads that our contacts recalled Dr. Neville having to park his car and ride in on horseback to make house calls and tend sick folks. In 1959 the first paved road through the Betty's Creek valley was completed, and the community was no longer iso-lated—or shielded—from the rapidly changing out-side world. Electricity, plumbing, and telephones followed and proved themselves to be agents of tremendous transformation in the everyday lives of people up and down the valley. Families who had once seen very little money in a year's time and had lived by what they raised in crops and livestock found themselves stunned by ever-increasing economic pressures and seeing chil-dren and grandchildren forced to seek their living outside of the community. Accessibility brought attention to the land on Betty's Creek, and the new and confusing issues of land development arose as property taxes increased and family properties began to change hands.

Our attempts to quantify what we were discov-ering took the form of tracing ever-growing family trees, searching out census figures and livestock and crop production statistics, and making graphs of land use.

In Laurie's conclusion to our study she wrote:

"It's hard to make specific conclusions in sorting out the various forces that now shape Betty's Creek and thousands of communities like it. It is decidedly unrealistic to entertain the notion of freezing an area, or trying to stop change completely. Certainly change can be a healthy, positive and enlightening course.

"The problem seems to lie in change that is disorganized and uncontrolled. Positive change ought to be, has to be ordered. When a community's development is the victim of a hundred different adverse pulls instead of being determined by the collective desires of the people, the resulting changes are bound to be, at the very least, disconcerting, and probably negative. It is here, at least in the overdevelopment of land and resources, that city and county government can reach its peak of importance in legislating to control disorder and negative change. City and county planning committees and well-executed zoning laws can help prevent or alleviate negative and disordered situations where local land development is involved.

"These positive instruments can only be wielded, however, when the majority of the people make themselves aware of the dangers and organize to meet them. This presents at least one real answer regarding the question of coping with change positively within a community."

Mounds of organized interviews, photographs and material, originally planned to be centerfolds in four separate issues of *"The Foxfire Magazine,"* could not be broken up into separate sections. MARBARLA was in total agreement: this study had to be one, entire issue.

Laurie was out of town when Mary and I took our concerns to Wig. He balked for well-calculated reasons:

1. He had promised inserts to subscribers.

2. An entire issue would put other ready-for-press issues on hold.

3. It wasn't fair to other students who had articles ready to go.

4. The budget just couldn't afford a whole separate issue.

We left the office devastated, but not defeated. Retreating to a tiny hole-in-the-wall restaurant, Mary fiddled with melting ice in a weak soda, "Boy, Wig was ticked big time: What are we going to do?"

The next day we told Laurie about our meeting with Wig and his decision. She simply said, "Of course it will be an issue." Her Mom had always said she was an obstinate child, and she took her stubborn, immovable self in for a second round.

Nervously, Wig drummed his pencil on the counter, glancing out the window, wishing for fresher air. After much heated debate he said, "I hate people who stand up for their convictions." Tension gave way to laughter; it was done. He was proud we practiced what he preached.

Later he commented, "Subsequent Foxfire students have never matched the sustained involvement in current social issues of the MARBARLA group."

The "Betty's Creek" issue sold out. It was never included in the many volumes of Foxfire books. Perhaps they felt it should stand alone.

THE HAMBIDGE CENTER
P.O. BOX 33
RABUN GAP, GEORGIA 30568

March 12, 1975

Mary Thomas,
Barbara Taylor, &
Laurie Brunson
FOXFIRE MAGAZINE
Rabun Gap, Georgia

Dear Mary, Barbara, and Laurie:

I want to take this opportunity to commend you on the fine, in-depth research job you did to come up with the current Betty's Creek Issue of Foxfire. It's a first rate job of recording a portrait of an area...it's past, present and it's aspirations for the future.

We will use it and refer to it over and over again as a guide to our own deepening involvement and commitment in the community. It will be immensely helpful to us in facilitating community interaction as an aid to finding areas of common concern and helping us all to discover alternatives for action wihch the community members might wish to pursue individually and together where the general interest is served.

It has already been helpful to us at the Hambidge Center in focussing on and defining our role in the community. The community itself will be our guide.Once the decision for deeper involvement was made, a decision which our interview helped spur, we have done a lot of thinking about how the Hambidge Center might best serve the community. The Betty's Creek issue you put together points to many directions for us to explore with our neighbors. The realization that so many of the residents are concerned for the future of this valley is heartening. The problem is beginning to be defined. One just first know that there is a problem and recognize the nature of it then discovering ones options becomes easier and more purposeful and one's actions become more cohesive.

Thank you for your excellent contribution in giving us an overview, background material and some thoughtful beginnings in defining the problem. We feel proud to be a part of the very special place that is Betty's Creek.

As we sponsor community meetings and gatherings for various purposes we will invite you and sincerely hope you will be able to attend and continue and expand your own personal identifications with and interest in the Betty's Creek community.

Best wishes to you.

Sincerely,

Mary

Mary Nikas

"...BUT WHEN IT IS SOWN IT GROWS UP..."

As Foxfire expanded in the early 1970s and its collection of priceless artifacts and recordings grew with it, the Foxfire student staff began to share a vision for a museum to house that collection. When Foxfire was offered free land by a local merchant because he felt Foxfire would enhance his tourist business, Wig presented that possibility to the class. The students rejected the offer hands down. We wanted to pay our own way, though we had no idea how the museum would support itself apart from the county's heavy tourist industry. The decision was made in 1973, to purchase land with royalty moneys from book sales. A fourteen-year-old student staff member signed the check. Foxfire became the owner of 110 acres on Black Rock Mountain, just above Mountain City, and 5 acres of land nearby on Highway 441.

The first building brought in and reconstructed on Foxfire land by students' hands was an old gristmill we had learned about from our beloved Aunt Arie. Other carefully reconstructed buildings followed, including a one-room log cabin originally built in 1820 that housed three generations of ten children each.

The Foxfire Museum and Heritage center was born.

During this same period a fire damaged the public high school in Clayton, and a short time later Rabun County voters passed a referendum to build a large, consolidated high school. Community students attending Rabun Gap-Nacoochee School would be bused 15 miles south to the new school. Families in northern Rabun County mourned the passing of an era and their close, longstanding relationship with the school Andrew Ritchie founded. Kids wondered what it was going to be like to be going to school with the students who had been their archrivals for so many years.

The change threw Foxfire into its own deep valley of decision. Rabun Gap-Nacoochee School had proven to be a positive medium for the conception, birth, and growth of a unique experiment in learning. The mix of mountain-born community students and curious, enthusiastic boarding students had been tremendously fruitful. Wig knew, however, that Foxfire ultimately had to go with the community. When the new high school opened, Foxfire was there, and continues to operate there today.

Over the past forty-five years many advancements and changes have been made in the Foxfire organization. "The Foxfire Approach to Teaching and Learning" program was developed and flourished in thirty-eight states and is now continued through Foxfire's Partner in Education, Piedmont College. Thousands of teachers have used the "Core Practices" to teach their own students in the Foxfire manner.

Over $25,000 in scholarships are awarded annually to local Rabun County Foxfire students, administered by Foxfire's Community Board Scholarship Committee. To date, over $850,000 has been awarded. Our daughter, Melissa, benefited from those scholarships.

Ann Henslee Moore is an Appalachian native and current Foxfire President and Executive Director. Mountain customs and traditions were part of her everyday life in Rabun County, making Ann a perfect choice to fan the fire in Foxfire. She was only ten years old when Foxfire was founded. After graduating from Rabun Gap-Nacoochee in 1974, Foxfire hired Ann as bookkeeper two years later. The rest is history. She has been with the organization 35 years. According to Bible mathematics, 35 means hope. Her heart is filled with faith, hope and charity. Ann has devoted all of her adult life to the work of Foxfire.

It is amazing that a small magazine started by an English class at Rabun Gap-Nacoochee School, in the North Georgia Mountains, is still in publication today-much to the credit of Ann's strong love and leadership.

A few months ago I stood in line at the Piggly Wiggly. A light tap on my shoulder gained my attention. I turned and saw behind me an early Foxfire contact. I was overjoyed as we embraced in reunion. She said, "I will never forget you and Foxfire. After a set of interviews were completed with my husband, he suffered a bad heart attack. We had just financed a new cook stove and worried how in the world we were going to pay for it. You came to our house with the loan paper stamped "paid in full."

I had long forgotten being part of that act of kindness.

"WHATEVER YOUR HAND FINDS TO DO, DO IT WITH ALL YOUR MIGHT..."

Ecclesiastes 9:10

Rabun Gap-Nacoochee's Biology teacher, Mr. Stiles, encouraged work. He said, "I don't care if you chose to dig ditches; be the best ditch digger around, and you won't be digging ditches long."

Rabun County had little choice of employment except a few textile mills or the tourist industry. Local kids that left for college generally took jobs in other places, working their entire lives in hopes of someday coming home. I could not conceive of leaving the mountains. If staying meant I'd have to peck poop with the chickens, so be it.

Dad had begun to work at the carpet mill long before Laurie and I took jobs there. He was a security guard, trading in his overalls for uniforms. Mama spent hours starching and ironing shiny seams in his work clothes that looked like she sewed them into place. They crackled like paper as he took them from perfectly placed hangers. A black-billed guard cap sported a shiny silver badge that set off his jet-black hair. Rain, shine, sleet, or snow, Dad had to be at his post of duty. Icy weather found him underneath his pickup hooking snow chains together, Mama saying, "If a dog pees on a tire it would spin."

A fond childhood memory is the employee Christmas party given by the plant. Dad would get tickets in early December. The dusty air inside the mill was transformed by smells of popcorn, oranges, candy, and cookies. After the party, plant officials handed out large gift bags to every kid.

The small mill was sold to a larger company. Twenty sprawling acres were placed under roof. Rabun Gap-Nacoochee School's horticulture class planted groves of loblolly pines that kept production areas hidden from the main road.

More waste-settling ponds were needed and placed on our Kelly's Creek road. They were surrounded by a chain-link fence. Dyes and chemicals were filtered there before the contents were spilled into the Little Tennessee River basin. Strong sulfuric odors tainted mountain air and spread through the area. We dreaded passing by enroute to town. Mama said, "Step on it, Jim! Lordy, this place stinks. Does it smell like that inside? I do declare, the whole crowd let loose gas and some messed their drawers. If that stink settles on us, we can't wash it off; floorboard the gas pedal. It can't be healthy."

Over a period of forty years the plant changed hands several times. Business moved south leaving unemployment and industrially blighted land and water.

Laurie and I worked at the mill for a few years. The wonderful co-workers made it tolerable. When working the graveyard shift, I lived on cornflakes. It messed up the natural routine and order of rest. I grew weary of the graveyard shift and the atmosphere created by a hard taskmaster. Before I quit, I had a job prospect in a big tourist resort already established.

In 1969 a huge cow pasture on nearby Scaly Mountain had crawled with different feet. Giant earth-moving machines walked about with mouthfuls of green pasture and leafy shade trees. The waters that flowed down to the beautiful Estatoah Falls, named for a Cherokee village, turned into rushing red mud, like foaming blood streaming from the ancient, punctured mountain-sides. Peaceful scenes were converted into Georgia's first ski resort, Sky Valley.

Distant breathtaking views sold the steep rugged lots. Artificial wonderlands were created to attract wealthy thrill seekers who were targeted to become residents in Alpine houses. Our quiet existence just underneath the once calm silence of Scaly Mountain was unsettled by constant winter roars of giant snowmaking machines. We were close enough to hear the machines, but the activity just over the top of the mountain we could not see. One had to drive down Kelly's Creek Road, turn right onto State highway 246 then go about four miles to get to the guarded entrance gate.

Gated resorts are offensive to Appalachian people. They send a clear message that newcomers want nothing to do with mountain neighbors. We know what boldly painted "Exclusive" signs mean.

Local people were tolerated as servants. Busboys and waitresses tended the multi-sided Alpine lodge decorated with black-and-white cowhides. I joined the housekeeping department in the mid-1980s.

During ski season the Sky Valley maintenance

Sample of a gated Community

department made sure Volkswagen vans were equipped with snow chains and ready to haul maids up dangerous winter roads. I was one of the drivers loaded with precious cargo: friends. I shudder at the risks taken on narrow, crooked, steep roads blanketed with natural snowfall. Some of the driveways were so steep the vans slid backwards. A tiny slip of the clutch could send us head over heels down steep ravines. It was pretty scary. From the snow covered rental porches, I looked down on Dad's gentle farm watching for chimney smoke circling like a wreath.

The end of winter ski season was the beginning of spring golf season. The Alpine lodge buzzed with an older crowd dressed in funny colored breeches and spiked shoes. I recall a resort golfer and property owner who ventured down the mountain, clad in pink golfing breeches to speak to Dad concerning the tin roof on the old barn. It interfered with his view. Curling his sand-tempered, lowlander toes in flip-flop sandals he asked, "If I buy the paint, will you paint that roof?" Dad's face became like a pressure cooker fixing to blow. His gauge was in the red zone. Sharp chinquapin eyes glowed like fire. "When hell freezes over! Feller, that barn was here before you were, and it will be here long after you are gone."

One hot summer day Dad was at the spring box resting and sipping cool water from a hewn gourd dipper when a long black Suburban pulled into the yard. Dark tinted windows concealed the passengers. Four doors opened, spitting out four men. Clicking locks followed their exit as they approached Dad. They looked like fancy television preachers—the kind dressed to kill while talking about One who wore the dress of a slave; the kind who live in million-dollar houses and talk about One who didn't have a place to lay His head.

Dad listened to them as he tapped the yellow gourd dipper dry. "You can't pack enough one-hundred bills in ten of your panel wagons to buy this place. When you can make snow in August, y'all come back to see me." Home has no price; they never returned.

Our beloved housekeeping supervisor at Sky Valley worked along beside us making ready a playground for the rich. Her dedication extended into late hours, and sometimes in the winter crews stayed the night because state roads that led home were closed. We developed a family kinship and held her dedication in high regard.

In 1988 management gave her an impossible ultimatum—either contract the cleaning or resign. She was devastated, being a sole breadwinner with two children. The astronomical start-up cost of contracting services made it impossible for her to remain. When one hurts, we all hurt. The entire housekeeping department walked off the job in protest. An office lady who prepared our walking papers said, "Loyalty won't buy a loaf of bread. Don't bite the hand that feeds you." Well, that depends on what is being fed. At our fired supervisor's small apartment, she told us she was deeply moved by our loyalty, love, and support, but she encouraged each of us to return, knowing jobs were scarce. We never looked back.

When you can't find a job, you make one. I decided to start my own business doing what so many people dislike doing.

"RABUN'S FIRST AND FINEST"

You might have guessed, Mama had a big case of OCD. She would not leave any job half done. "Anything worth doing is worth doing right." Everything she laid hands to was perfected to the best of her ability. After a full day of washing clothes on Mondays, Tuesdays were reserved for starching and ironing. It was common for her to spend hours on Dad's work uniforms that hung like slick ribbons on a sturdy nail.

Twice a year, while Dad was at work, she smeared the wood floors with Johnson's paste wax. We pulled the wool socks that Granny Lou made over our shoes for a night of skating fun.

I assembled mop buckets, ragbags, vacuum cleaners, and tote trays inside a Ford Pinto before the first client called for house-cleaning service. My operating capital was faith and hope. Mama jested, "Well, if it don't work, you can always eat the Pinto."

Word of mouth is the best advertisement. Soon I was able to hire valued assistance as the business grew in leaps and bounds. My precious sister-in-law, Debra, returned from the University of Georgia to become a shoulder-to-shoulder partner. Together we worked at perfecting a speed-cleaning system for crews with quality first, production second.

I recall my introduction of work aprons going over like a rock. I reasoned that no one hired a carpenter to build a house without one. "If you need it, have it by your side." Each team member made one trip around each room. Dead raisins or stubborn pancake batter on countertops were quickly cleaned with convenient tools from the apron. They even had a plastic-lined pocket for stashing scattered debris. The aprons proved to be invaluable and made our work easier. A crew of three could master general cleaning of ten or more houses a day.

DOO kept the Pinto running, saying it was made out of pasteboard and stuck together with bubble gum. We pulled the transmission in and out so many times he said, "Let's put a zipper on it." Once I crawled out from underneath its blue frame, dirty and oily, to answer the phone. After the voice on the other end gained information about our services she asked, "Are you black?" I looked at my arms and said, "Why, yes, I am right now, but it will wash off." She hung up.

Our crew strove to fulfill a genuine community need. Changing times kept many families busy working outside the home. For these, hiring a cleaning company became a necessity. It was the full-time residents who kept bread on our tables. The second-home owners on area lakes and in local resorts were icing on the cake.

A book could not hold all our many experiences and encounters, both negative and positive. One patron tried to pay us with sacks of crumpled beer cans sitting near his shiny Mercedes. Another offered as tips moldy bread and cakes. I replied in common colloquiums, "This stuff is ruin't." The patron said, "Oh, no, it isn't burnt." I spelled it for her: R-U-I-N-E-D = "ruin't."

Mountain people call fruit flies "drunkards." I advised a lady she had drunkards in her kitchen. She wanted to know who let them in.

I am still misunderstood, but its fun.

Wig's warnings about mountain people being stereotyped became a personal reality. We were saddened that some patrons really thought us depraved and ignorant. We will never forget the lady who counted each item, including canned goods, after we left. To question Appalachian honesty is a grave insult, and one false accusation would sink us. She was dropped like a hot potato.

Another patron who owned a national motel chain spoke in a degrading manner about cleaning people. Debra quickly responded, "If it were not for maids keeping your rooms clean, you'd not be up here swinging high-heeled shoes on the end of painted toe nails, looking out over poor, uneducated, stupid people's lands. Have a nice day, lady."

For every unpleasant encounter, however, there were scores of patrons who blessed us through trust, support, advice, encouragement, gifts and appreciation.

The highest compliment I value is trust. Recently a long-time Lake Rabun patron said by phone, "I was meeting with my Atlanta colleagues and mentioned I had never seen the lady who cleans my house on Lake Rabun. They were shocked by that amount of trust. You came highly recommended and that was enough for me."

Dr. Bob Wells, a retired surgeon from Atlanta and his lovely wife Ruth West, a retired lawyer are long-time Foxfire fans and transplants from Atlanta. I had heard about their volunteer work as child advocates long before they requested my cleaning services for their Betty's Creek home. They always give me a blank check. I am touched by their great confidence and trust.

Dr. Bob said, "I first came to Rabun County in the mid 30s, when I was seven years old, to Camp Dixie. I loved the mountains then and I love them now. I always wanted to be back whenever I could. About 1975 I bought property on Lake Rabun. Years later when Ruth fell in love with the Betty's Creek area we decided to move up here. Ruth is on the board of directors at the Hambidge Art Center and melted into the sights and sounds of nature's voice. She remembers driving up Betty's Creek road and saying 'O my God! This is where I belong.'

"I came home from a trip in about 2003. Ruth met me at the airport and said, 'Guess what I did while you were gone? I bought a house on Betty's Creek!' Our home is the old estate of Claude and Edith Darnell, former employees of the Hambidge Art Center. Our wonderful neighbors are the fourth generation of the early Justice settlers.

"A lot of Hambidge Center artists say there is tremendous energy here. We enjoy just being quiet in the middle of endless beauty.

"The Center owns about 620 acres and is a big part of preserving Betty's Creek. Like any organization sometimes it runs low on money and the directors try to figure out a way to keep things afloat and from time to time somebody will suggest selling land. Luckily so far, the vast majority say NO WAY! Once land is gone, it's hard to redeem. Selling land is a poor way to solve money problems."

Dr. Bob said, "I won't ever get tired of looking at the mountains. I'm in my 80s and wonder how much time I've got left, without dwelling on it too much. I expect at my age Betty's Creek is not going to change too much. I'd like to see growth controlled, but a special place, you are not going to keep it exactly the same. There is an old saying, "I'm on board, Jack, pull up the ladder, don't let anyone else up here." We are just glad to be here. We have a place in Atlanta, but Betty's Creek is HOME."

Dr. Bob and Ruth are precious additions to the mountains.

Mt. Picken's Nose located on Betty's Creek

I met Chevin Woodruff around seven years ago at Clayton Presbyterian Church where she taught a Bible study class. Soon afterwards she moved the study to where she lived, a place she called Splendor Mountain Resort. The first time I drove out there, I was surprised. It did not look like a resort at all—in fact, I had to look hard to see the buildings.

Chevin: "I was living in Atlanta in a great old ranch-style home with one hundred year old oaks in the yard. I had lots of dogs. I thought it was okay to walk dogs off leash. There were laws against that. People would say, 'YOU SHOULD PUT YOUR DOGS ON A LEASH!' even though they stayed close beside me. I got in my car and set my speed odometer for fifty miles. Fifty miles from Atlanta did not get me to Rabun County but it did set wheels in motion...

"I made some real estate contacts within the fifty miles and learned about ten acres with a waterfall on Boggs Mountain in Rabun County that was just beginning to be developed. That waterfall seized my attention. My two poodles jumped out of the car, ran to the top and slid down. They returned to get my mother's dog. All three of them ran to the top and slid down the waterfall again. Immediately I said, 'I'll take it!' The real estate agent ran over and hugged a tree and then hugged me.

"My first intention was just a small cabin that I could use and walk my dogs on the weekend. I ended up buying more property and moving up here.

"I spent five years of walking the property,

praying for guidance that God's will be done. I have a passion for nature and not bruising the landscape. Thankfully, I met Madison McCracken, a neighbor and local pastor who had walked here all his life. He owns an environment-friendly excavation service. He was a God-send to Splendor Mountain."

Of the 75 acres Chevin purchased, only 20 acres have been developed. Splendor Mountain Resort has a meeting lodge with full restaurant-grade kitchen, a pavilion, and two guest lodges.

Chevin says, "It has been eleven years since Splendor Mountain Resort has been completed. Life here builds my faith and helps me endure."

One of my favorite patrons is Dorothy Ann King. Her family was among the first families from Atlanta to discover Lake Rabun about 1917 through a relative that was an Attorney with Georgia Power Company.

Dorothy's father first came to the lake in the womb of her Grandmother. He was an inventor. His Atlanta-based company kept him busy. Dorothy Ann said, "Dad couldn't leave Atlanta until he retired because of company responsibilities and working to pay taxes in Rabun County. He said, "You don't own the land, it's leased from the county."

An explosion of lake lovers in the 1970s caused available land to be a rare find. Dorothy recalls home owners went from about 30 with no security gates in the early days to presently over 400 with many gated driveways.

If ever a person melted into an environment it

is Dorothy Ann. She is the picture of the mountains that literally took possession of her:

"I was born in Atlanta but went to school in the flatlands of Cochran, Georgia. We started coming up to the mountains each week. I just felt an incredible sense of security here. I'm not religious at all but I liken the feeling to God holding us in HIS arms. Being here feeds something beyond comprehension and vision. Deep breaths of fresh air mix with great appreciation and the reality of true freedom fills me up. I have talked with many neighbors on the lake who say all worries and stress are dropped on the highway at the county line as they progress to the mountains.

"I love the feeling of security in these mountains. It is wonderfully rare to be able to leave your house unlocked or the keys in your truck just in case the neighbor might need something. Likewise neighbors did the same. Permission was unspoken, just a silent friendly agreement. You never felt you had to warn neighbors you were coming by, but just show up like family. That quality for the most part has vanished today.

"Another change I miss is small stores. Alley's Grocery was an icon on Lake Rabun for many years. He had ancient working gas pumps, old hornet nests, and honeycombs hanging in his store. You could get everything from fishing worms to daily newspapers. Mr. Alley is a great fellow. Recently he sold his little store and retired. He took so much more away than just himself. If customers came by without their wallet it was okay to come back tomorrow and pay. You can't do that at Wal-Mart.

"Nobody stops to help with roadside car trouble anymore, I miss that too.

"Lake Rabun, like the mountains, has become crowded; and with crowds come change. Another thing I really miss is pickup truck drivers don't wave anymore; heck they don't even keep the same truck too long. There is an element of kinship and personality in vehicles."

Dorothy's modest cabin is not lake side, by choice, but up a hard dirt road surrounded by tall trees, red clay banks and grassy fields where white-tail deer lower their heads munching red clover in total safety from the hunter's aim. Deer are a common sight.

Inside worn T-shirts, old jeans and weathered work boots is a deep still spirit like the area she loves. Sun shades (her signature) cover laughing eyes like green foliage shadow sleepy coves.

Motorists can observe Dorothy Ann mending fences, raking leaves or cutting grass on roadsides. Her Ford pickup truck rolls over lake property that has become gold dust to real estate companies. She is armed with shovels, rakes, chainsaws, weed-eaters, gasoline cans, and her beloved dog, Iggy sitting in the back like a King himself.

When I see her working I cannot resist stopping to chat. Even a short visit with Dorothy Ann is a sure-fine experience filled with life and laughter. She lifts a tanned face from working with a hearty greeting. Her settled spirit bears witness to total contentment that she finds in the smallest things. Wild ducks stop splashing to approach the lakeshore for a tossed lunch. Dragonflies bob up and down on soft ripples of calm waters.

Occasionally as we chat a trout breaks the still, blue water like the interrupting of a dream, but Dorothy is not a dreamer.

At day's end with well-earned rest and good coffee she admires magnificent views of the mountains that hold her here.

Dorothy is a friend to all unless you drive drunk around the lake, in which case she will shoot your tires off.

One of her neighbors told me, "If she says STOP you better hit the brakes." After he sobered up he appreciated Dorothy Ann's concern and called her a great friend.

She has never met a stranger. She will end her days on Lake Rabun, but as long as breath remains so will her compassion and volunteer work as an advocate for children. All things come to a halt for the sake of helping abused children in the county.

As for the future Dorothy Ann says, "I don't see any reason to leave here. I'd like to hang around for a hundred years. You can never tire of happiness."

We worked a lot on Lake Rabun among Atlanta's elite. Tucked at the end of a private road was one of the ugliest million-dollar-divorce suits ever. Husband and wife took turns using their lake house on weekends. One weekend, the wife left a white business card lying on the counter. It simply said, "Hired Killer" and a phone number. I sweated bullets, finally deciding to call the husband in his high-rise office, yelling, "DUCK!" On our way out we met Mountain Patrol. I explained what was happening. The officer split a gut, laughing. "It is an exterminating company!" Needless to say my face grew red with embarrassment, hot enough to light a cigarette from.

We worked hard, laughed much, and pampered the Ford Pinto while we prayed for a van with a heater.

Once, Mama accompanied me to check houses. Walking down a drive I heard scraping sounds behind me. Mama was pulling a brand new, twelve hundred dollar vacuum cleaner through the gravel. I yelled, "OH, NO! We carry that." She yelled back, "In case you are late finding out, the wheel has been invented. This heavy thing has some."

The chief way I and other small contractors advertised on area lakes was to nail small signs to already nail-infested trees. The county marshall's office called me one afternoon. "Barbara, you are in violation of county ordinances. You must have all cleaning signs off the lakes or be fined."

After removing the signs, I bought a copy of the Rabun County Official Zoning Ordinance and Subdivision Regulations, 2003, for review. I read the reason for sign placement ordinances: "To protect the health, safety, welfare, and general well-being of the citizens of Rabun County." The "general well-being and welfare" for small businesses such as mine depends on generating income for jobs and ultimately to pay county taxes. After reading a few more paragraphs I became "madder than a wet hen" because while it is not permitted for local services such as lawn care, stone masons, carpenters, electricians and cleaning services to place small signs in view of passing customers, it is permittcd for directional signs, real estate companies and politicians.

According to the Rabun County's Official Zoning Ordinance and Subdivision Regulations book, Article X111, page 80, "With these objectives and purposes in mind, it is the intention of this article to authorize the use of signs that: Are compatible with their surroundings in terms of zoning, existing land use, and architectural characteristics; Are appropriate to the type of activity to which they pertain; To afford the business community equal and fair opportunity to advertise and promote products and services without discrimination...."

I felt the ordinance was unfair.

At the end of twenty years of service, I decided to quit the cleaning business.

My hands-on Foxfire experiences proved to be better than a college education in business management. I created advertising flyers and business cards, arranged appointments and kept the books. Public relations are a big part of self-employment. I was supremely blessed by each mentor that empowered me with strength, encouragement, patience, faith, knowledge and pride during my young years.

We clean fish, too!

"For I Will Contend With Him Who Contends With You, And I Will Save Your Children"
Isaiah 49:25

Connie Taylor Moore is more of a daughter than a niece. She was introduced to "Rabun's First & Finest Cleaning Service" at an early age and worked faithfully for about twelve years until I sold the assets to her. She writes....

"My first recollection of Aunt Barbara is, she took me to the dime store and loaded me up with my young heart's desire. It wasn't Christmas or my birthday either! I was spoiled rotten. She and Uncle Larry lived within walking distance and were an easy escape with all my mini-woes and trials. Walking in her footsteps was/is a great challenge for any person. She instilled deep convictions in important things she believed in. Honesty, dependability, hard work and generosity are a few of her qualities. She was ever-present on job details in addition to being manager at the end of many hard days.

"As new owner of "Rabun's First & Finest" Cleaning Service I was constantly aware of her influence and undying pride in the business she had birthed.

"Continual growth would not allow me to personally accompany my crews on work details. That changed right away. I had to learn to trust my crew leaders to act in my stead.

"At that time I lived with my husband, Kenneth, about a mile down the road. We had all the material things one could ask for: a great income, a comfortable home, motor coach, swimming pool, new vehicles each year, dogs and cats...everything my heart desired.

"I suffered from occasional migraine headaches and became addicted to stadol. Stadol is a synthetic opiate, similar to liquid morphine. Aunt Barbara (and others) noticed a great change in me. I became withdrawn and evaded responsibilities. At one point she talked to my doctor about stopping my prescription. He did, but that led me to seek other illegal reliefs to feed my addiction. Drugs became my god. In short, they cost me everything I held dear: my husband, family, home, self-respect, and everything else. I lived for my next high. I would disappear for weeks at a time to hang with fellow users.

"I chose to sell my Kelly's Creek property in large part to feed my addictions. It went up in the smoke of cocaine.

"I was broke within a few months and I resented my parents for not giving me money which I would have used to support my habit. In short, nobody could stop the white dusty demon of cocaine that controlled my every moment. I put everyone who loved me through a literal hell. To keep his sanity my husband divorced me. My wonderful parents also gave up on me in all things except prayer. They rang the prayer bells in heaven constantly, crying out to God on my behalf. Even if they had lost me to the world beyond, their voice would continue to penetrate the universe that somehow, someway wherever I was, that God would reclaim my lost way.

"God heard. I was living in destitute conditions in another county without food for days. I woke up in a pool of clear vomit and began to cry out to God for deliverance. From the bottom of my self-created pit there was no way out but UP. The burden of shame was as great as the mighty withdrawal demons that turned my body inside out. I promised to never touch dope again if HE would let me live. HE sent an angel in the form of an elderly neighbor named Sue to my door with a dollar bag of orange circus peanut candy. That was my first food in many days. That day was a turning point for me. Today I celebrate 9 years of sobriety.

"Fractured trust is very hard to regain. One of the most touching and memorable moments I can recall: Shortly after I began recovery (on my own with God's help) I came one Christmas to visit Uncle Larry and Aunt Barbara. A wood fire crackled in the heater as a pan of water wobbled on top. The kitchen filtered seasonal smells from an overloaded table of food. I could have lapped it all up like a dog but fought the temptation and hid my hunger. Their trust, too, I had violated. I did not feel worthy to sit at their table. As I turned to leave, (and I will never ever forget this) Uncle Larry put down his remote control and arose from his chair. He opened his wallet and handed me $50. He said, "Go get you something." That act of kindness was great, but not as great as the evidence that he trusted me once again. He was the first to extend forgiveness. I love him for that. He helped me reclaim my self-respect and faith in mankind. His loving action helps keep me clean today because I cannot defile his big confidence in me.

"Sometime afterwards my fiancé's daughter gave birth to a beautiful baby girl who was addicted to meth. The doctors offered little hope that that baby would live. I remember falling to my knees begging God to allow me a chance to make restitution. I promised to raise Haley as my own and provide the same loving environment that I had experienced and defiled. HE granted my request. I took her home and held her tiny body as it cringed with withdrawal symptoms. With God's blessings and help she is now a happy recovered inspiration and God's gift to me. Every day is a miracle.

"When I drive up from White County, Georgia, to visit Kelly's Creek, the first reminder of community change is the wearing down of the mighty granite mountain at the quarry. When I was small it seemed to reach to the sky. On up the winding road the feeling of "home" vanishes. Litter taints the roadside where flowers bloomed. It's not the same. My family "holler" is now dotted with rentals. I pass strangers who never wave driving in the middle of the narrow road. A pure way of life seems to have vanished. I know in my heart if Grandpa was still around he would be sad about the invasions that changed home.

"I've had many battles with cancer. In the low times I'd close my eyes and return to the true in life. Memories sustain me."

* * *

During Connie's struggles I pondered many times why we poison our lives with pain, destruction, and artificial highs. It's especially tough to watch loved ones perish away. We feel powerless to bring them to sanity.

With defeated spirit and lowered head, I walked along a path pondering the fate of those I loved. My focus changed from the trodden path to a spot of poisoned earth sprayed with weed killer. In the midst of barren ground grew a mighty tree complete with extended limbs and lush foliage. For a moment I stood underneath its large shade looking at that poisoned spot, and hope returned.

The last thing ever lost is hope.

"OLD AGE IS A CROWN OF GLORY FOR DOING RIGHT"

A slower lifestyle did not last long. January 23, 1997, I took a less strenuous job at the local senior center. It provided county senior citizens much needed services like shopping assistance, transportation to medical appointments, hair styling, group outings, and group activities such as quilting. I reconnected with a few Foxfire contacts I had not seen in years.

The Meals on Wheels program offered wonderful opportunities to meet volunteer carriers and make lasting friendships. It was customary for me to accompany new volunteers on their first delivery routes.

Miss Ann Taylor came faithfully twice a week to run the longest delivery route. We loaded meal canisters into the back of her ancient white Ford Courier pickup truck. Traces of gray moss on the glove box matched two neatly-folded quilts stacked in the center of the seat. I soon learned Miss Ann felt she had more important things to spend money on than a replacement heater for her truck. She spent extra time with lonely shut-in clients. During holidays she postponed her own celebrations to deliver hand-made gifts and cheerful holiday greetings. Her heart was as big as Dixie. Over time she became a frequent visitor in our home and she and I shared dreams and drama.

She had struggled with reading and tests and was labeled a "slow learner" in elementary school. In high school she was told not to even bother applying to go to college. She graduated from the University of Georgia with a B.S in education and from Indiana University with a M.S in physical education/health. When she was in her 50s she discovered she had dyslexia.

She was the proud owner and director of one of the oldest summer camps in the United States, Camp Dixie. Miss Ann represented all that Camp Dixie was founded upon in 1914.

Miss Ann and her mother were looking to buy a camp, and they visited Camp Dixie in 1969. The spiritual resonance and Biblical symbolism she felt and perceived when she drove in convinced her that she was meant to buy the 350-acre camp. Miss Ann was only 29 years old when she took on the full responsibility of Camp Dixie and its future. She never considered herself the owner—she saw herself as the guardian of the spiritual legacy that had been passed down for more than 50 years. She passionately believed in the camp's purpose and in the seven principles originally established by its founder: Physically Robust, Mentally Strong, Politically Sound, Domestically True, Vocationally Correct, Morally Brave, and Spiritually Deep. She put the profits back into the camp and drove a school bus to make ends meet.

I think Miss Ann was practicing the "Morally Brave" principle when she was hit with demands from county officials that she drill an expensive well. For years she had piped pure spring water for the camp to use. She submitted test after certified test proving the water and its source was pure. She offered to buy bottled drinking water for the campers, but the local officials insisted the well must be drilled. The hits kept coming, and I saw how heavy her heart was with concern for the future of Camp Dixie.

The blow that literally broke her heart was the threat by county authorities to close Camp Dixie down. Her final words to her business assistant and spiritual daughter Rhonda Conrad were, "We don't have to take this." Ann dropped to her kitchen floor with a massive heart attack.

My phone rang after Miss Ann was flown to a bigger hospital. Rhonda's shaky voice said, "We need a miracle. Miss Ann is in critical condition." DOO and I drove to the hospital to find our friend bound by plastic tubes and needles. We joined hands and petitioned God for His best for Miss Ann.

As DOO and I drove home in the late afternoon, a beautiful rainbow appeared over Camp Dixie. I knew it was the promise that Miss Ann would be camping in a much better place.

Rhonda Conrad and husband Jason Airlie keep her memory alive and Camp Dixie's flame glowing bright. With the exception of a few modernizations, the camp has remained pretty much the same for nearly 100 years. The spiritual and moral emphasis, the principles, the atmosphere, the activities all hark back to the beginning.

Rhonda observed, "We had our 95th reunion in 2009 and the alumni came expecting great change. They were amazed that we kept Camp

Dixie the same all these years. Most of them head straight for the open-air chapel. They just sit praying or thinking about the values held dear from their Camp Dixie experience. I hope Camp Dixie will always be a safe haven for all our Camp family."

Land developers are invading areas bordering camp property. Increased traffic on the main road became a safety hazard to campers crossing to go to the stables, but changing times bring pressing concerns for campers on a different level: "It is easy here to be your best self. The challenge is when they go home. Will they remember the seven principles of Dixie?"

Rabun County senior citizens coveted and had earned two major things: loafing and laughing. Together we did both. At times I chauffeured the van, known as the Big Cheese, wherever they wanted to go. Elders deserve double honors; they were my bosses.

Miss Mae Craig was picked up three times a week from her small apartment in a Government housing project. At eighty years of age she was spunky and full of life, sharp as a tack with unmatched humor.

One summer afternoon she expressed a longing to return to her old home place under Glassy Mountain. Word was passed among seniors: "We're going home with Mae; all aboard the Big Cheese." Miss Mae's reminiscing prepared our minds to enter the past along the way.

An old farmhouse at the end of a grassy field was just as she described. We stepped off the van into the world of her youth. An ever-present breeze brought scents from an apple orchard across the road. Masses of lilacs bloomed in the old homestead beds.

Miss Mae sat on the remains of the old porch, unloading memories forever etched in her heart. The glow on her face was as refreshing as a summer shower that settles trodden paths. As she talked, we could sense the presence of family, expecting her mother to appear in the old doorway announcing supper time; her dad rearing his sweaty head with an attentive ear from the woodpile in the back. When the carnal ear is turned off, we can hear with our heart. Have you ever noticed, "ear" is the center word in "heart"?

I heard happy, playful voices of children, tumbling in tall pasture grass beyond the old locust fence; and Miss Mae in her very own playhouse, a flat rock under a mighty oak tree.

Tubs of farm produce had sagged long porch benches from an era of self-sufficiency and plenty to eat. "One good thing about growing your own food, you knew what you were eating."

An old well was surrounded with flowering vines, reminiscent of the deep blessings of cool water shared freely on hot days and friends who were like that good drinking water-always there.

It was a vanished lifestyle without worldly goods, yet richer than my generation would ever know. It was hard to leave. In the rear view mirror, I watched Miss Mae glue her eyes in a final survey as we drove away. The old home place disappeared from sight, but never from our minds. I treasure that memory and feel blessed to be counted worthy to absorb great wisdom and share yesteryear with those who experienced it.

An old shed on Miss Mae's home place

My aging parents were not tempted to join us at the senior center saying, "We get homesick at home." After work I would stop to check on them and share events of the day. They enjoyed hearing about their senior friends. Usually, Mama was busy in the kitchen while Dad watched his new satellite television. Mama said, "Look up yonder in th' turnip patch at that big white pancake pointed towards the elements. There ain't enough syrup in Georgia to cover that thing."

The preacher stopped by quite often. He

believed antennas were the devil's horns hooked to the house. He said, "Well, Cleo, I hear you can get over one-hundred channels to watch." Mama replied, "I don't even know how to turn th' thing on, but we don't get but two channels around here; the rasslin' and the Playboy." Her jesting almost caused the preacher to pass out cold as a wedge.

It was common for folks to come by just to watch television with Dad. Mama was in the kitchen filling a pan with water. A news clip reported wildfires burning in California. Uncle Millard said, "Look at that fire on the television!" Quicker than a cat's wink, Mama bounded from the kitchen with a full pan of water, emptying it completely on Dad's new attraction. Smoke filled the room. The television drowned. Dad said, "You've played hell now!"

I have no doubt that the first stages of Alzheimer's disease were occurring, yet it was hard to tell exactly because of her spontaneous and comical nature. My first big clue something was wrong: She poured blue liquid into a drinking glass and was about to swallow it. "What's that?" I asked. She said, "Kool-aid." I knew she never bought that. It was mouthwash and a big red flag.

Dad's health was failing, but he kept an eye on her actions. Most of his days were spent in his armchair near the wood heater. Traditional Knapp work boots sat in the corner as he waited for an ingrown toenail to heal, which never did. The doctor removed the toe. Clogged leg veins blocked healing blood flow. We drove him to the hospital twice a day for strong antibiotic treatments. Each time he begged not to go. "They are burning me up with medicine." He only got worse and depended on a walker to get around.

The family took turns caring for our aging parents. Brother Ellis kept wood on the porch and the fire going inside. Ernest brought hot food each day. Bea took up any slack. Occasionally, I spent the night.

Mama and I sat in the living room, watching out the window as a full moon began its journey over early spring-tipped mountains, dispelling the darkness. I asked, "Do you think man has walked on the moon?" She said, "Why would a' body wanna do that? Your Daddy said they left a junk car up there. I hope they parked it in gear; it might coast off on us. Granny Lou said a man was put up there for burning brush on Sunday. See his smoke in the face of the moon?"

Dad's voice broke our conversation from his rear bedroom. "Cleo, I want to get up and kneel down to pray." Raising her voice so he could hear, she said, "No, you ain't. We can't get you back in th' bed; just pray where you are."

A second request was made: "I feel lower than HIS feet; I wanta get up and kneel down." The sound of his straight chair moving on the floor told me he had managed to get up without any assistance.

I neared his room, but stopped short to listen. Dad was in better hands. A humble heart poured forth simple words. The house was filled with Divine presence. Reality is touchable. Reality is Christ, the secret inside. Dad interceded for his family and friends with a sure value of each one.

Two wills were joined together that none should perish. Not once did he ask for healing nor try to persuade God to change HIS mind. It was all about others. There was a moment of golden silence. I heard and felt love on its knees.

The next day we prepared for another trip to the hospital and more "burn me up medicine." He moved slowly down the ramp built by neighbors. Loosing his hands from the cold metal walker, he placed them on the banister in a lingering fashion. The setting sun streaked bright rays across earthen fields. Dad learned by watching the soil. We, too, are dust of the earth. With a long sigh he seemed to loose plough lines in his mind. Dim eyes rose above a small patch of tasseling corn as he focused on the ancient hills that gave him birth. Harvest was near; he was looking beyond.

A hummingbird needled sweet nectar from the Rose of Sharon tree blooming in the yard. We watched as it flew home. Dad said, "This time I won't be back." My head denied his words; my heart knew the truth. July 12, 1997, we gathered at the hospital. Mama did not grasp what was happening. I was sorta glad for the cloak of protection. Dad passed on to his reward.

Aunt Mary Carpenter was older than Dad, her only brother. She came from Scaly Mountain to Hunter's Funeral Home for visitation. She was a strong tower and support for Dad all his life. Feebly, she approached casket side. Placing warm hands on cold ones, she said, "Jim, my brother, I told you to wait until I could go with you, but you couldn't. I will be along soon. You beat me to Heaven."

The gravesite dirt was covered with plastic green grass. The casket rested above a hole that could never hold Dad. Mama saw, but did not perceive. She came home and washed clothes.

Over a three-year period, Mama grew progressively worse, yet her humor stayed intact. We stocked her shelves with plenty of food, awaiting the much talked-about millennium bug in the year 2000. She said, "They talk like some kind of bug is comin' through here. I hope it likes pinto beans; we've plenty of 'em."

Sister Bea hired day care; at night we took turns keeping her comfortable as the disease stole her away deeper into a dark tunnel. Mama was becoming an empty shell. Very early one morning, I heard movements in the kitchen, then tapping sounds. She was attempting to break a ceramic egg on a cold frying pan. I asked, "Are you all right?" She answered, "Yeah, but there is sure as hell something wrong with that hen!" I rolled in the floor laughing.

The day arrived when we could do no more. Nursing home discussion divided the family. We knew if the tables were turned, she would never commit our care to someone else. That made the decision much tougher. I reasoned that special care was an act of love. Christ sets our example. HE committed his mother to the care of another at the cross.

Mama was never religious, but she knew Jesus. Despite total memory loss, she never forgot HIM and prayed each night. I thought about HIS promise, "I will never leave you..." The preacher went to visit at the nursing home. He talked across the table at Mama about Heaven's golden streets and pearly gates. "Cleo, you wanna go to Heaven don't you?" She asked, "Are you going?" The preacher said, "O Hallelujah! Yes!" Mama paused, "Well, if you are going, I believe I'll just stay here, and if you intend to drive that car, it won't make it." I laughed until my sides hurt. Mama was in great spiritual shape.

In January 2003 doctors told us she had an aneurism. Time was short. With heavy hearts again, we gathered around a sad bedside. Bending low I took her hand and softly sang her favorite hymn in her ear.

"O precious is the flow
That makes me white as snow
No other fount I know
Nothing but the blood of Jesus"

Her chest rose and fell its final time in this realm. Tear ducts opened from a severely dehydrated body. Our tears mixed with hers. Bea dried Mama's last tears with her hand and closed her once lively eyes, January 17, 2003. Seventeen means victory.

DOO drove us home through glistening snow before daybreak. Frozen flakes sparkled like diamonds hanging on trees. A moving object in the sky seized my attention. I pointed it out to my very skeptical husband. He agreed it looked like a bird in slow motion. The object was too compelling to dismiss and keep driving. He pulled off the road to get a better view. We watched the bright form

Mama
1918—2003

ascend the mountain range, drifting eastward. To lighten the moment, DOO said, "I didn't know Heaven was over that way." It was a sign of comfort sent especially for us. The Holy Spirit took the form of a dove in the Bible. HE is our comforter.

Part III

"IT'S NOT MY MOUNTAIN ANYMORE"

One Tomorrow: By Melissa Woodall

My Grandparents were important parts in my daily life teaching with love and humor throughout their days. Probably their greatest concern was getting to town once a month to buy staples like sugar, flour, salt and soda. When they got home I recall Grandpa squinting over the register receipt accounting for each item before it joined his huge collection stored in a well-kept wooden box. Granny kept "a sweetie drawer" filled with bite-size Almond Joy candy bars as quick rewards.

I have many fond memories of them. One Christmas while my Grandparents were away at church I saw the opportunity for a few dollars and cut their small spruce pines to sell for Christmas trees. I ended up having to pay with my own labor, helping Grandpa carry firewood from his old shed into the house. He tripped over a board. I remember thinking he would never hit the ground because he seemed so tall, but he did and got right back up with the firewood still in his arms. "No use picking it up twice."

Another venture was, I cut about twenty stalks of his prized corn for a play fort. He was not happy but decided on a forgiving hug and a promise not to do it again.

In their day I was free to roam the countryside on foot or bicycle as the community was formed with watchful family members. Back then, my greatest danger was a snake or getting stung by a bee. Now, increased traffic and unknown neighbors hamper that freedom for my ten year old son, Sterling. I never knew the evils in the world until I left home and took a job in the area as a social worker with child protective services.

Social services in Grandpa's day were much different. The community took care of needs and the unruly. The men folks got together and paid the transgressor a warning visit. If he did not take heed they tied him on a rail, carried him down the road and dumped him. He called it, "Loving your neighbor on a rail." He believed in taking care of your family.

Grandpa told me about a family who borrowed a cow. When the head of the household died, the owner of the cow reclaimed her. The neighbors approached the cow's owner saying, "Now, that widow and younguns need that cow. If you can spare her...take her back." That same day the cow returned along with enough hay for the winter. Neighborhood discipline is replaced by government.

Case workers are like the police. We are generally hated until we're needed. The hardest part of this job is the abused children. I've seen the innocent suffer the torments of hell being born addicted to whatever drug the mother was on. I am haunted by one case where the parent was permitted to use narcotic drugs for a variety of reasons during pregnancy in addition to dabbling in illegal drug abuse. These transgressions almost always impact the newborn for the duration of their lives.

I have seen infants born exposed to and positive for methamphetamine. One lay in a neonatal unit for nearly two months hooked to monitors and labored to stay alive. She underwent surgery to repair and replace her lungs, trachea, and stomach as the meth had burned holes through out her digestive and respiratory system. She was rendered disabled at the tender age of three. Her mother went on to have four more children with similar conditions.

Most of the public has no idea what goes on in an addict's home. Most children are severely malnourished and dehydrated as their parents have neglected to provide food and water because illegal drugs come first. I recall one toddler who was restrained in a car seat for days, strapped, while the mother was passed out on the floor. He had third degree burns around his neck and arms.

I am very fortunate to have good parents. As far back as I can remember, my parents were (are) a steady constraint in our lives. (Most kids haven't had that.) Daddy's black dinner bucket laced with quarry dust sat on the table awaiting the next day's sandwich. After working all day making little rocks out of big ones he carried me on strong dusty shoulders through the woods exploring nature's trails.

His eyes reflect a heart full of love. He might not give friends a hug or verbalize, "I love you," but he will fill their woodshed or pantry or meet any need he possibly can. Words are less powerful than action, but both mark a charitable man.

News commentators would be out of a job around Daddy because he speaks plain and simple. Others are never left wondering what he said or what he meant. He is quick to temper over and defend his family even when we don't deserve it. I recall a bus fight, which I started, resulting in my drawers getting torn. Mama usually planned her words well. That is not Daddy's nature. He called the grade school right away. "Look here Oscar Cook; my youngun came home with drawers tore, and it damn well better not happen again." I can hear Mr. Cook laughing at Daddy's manner, but he got the job done. I have not had to call him to war as an adult, but I am beyond confident that a simple instruction would land the assailant in dire circumstances—the wrath of my Daddy.

Mom inherited a creative imagination that kept us entertained. When I was in first grade she told me we had leprechauns in our yard. I spent endless hours overturning rocks and prowling through the grass looking for little green men. She said, "O, they only come out at night to play in fairy city."

Adding to my adventure, she found a ceramic green man, placed him in the tall clover that she sprinkled with bits of "glow in the dark" cereal box toys. One night she gave me a Mason jar and took me outside to sneak up on "fairy city." I was amazed and breathless. She said, "Catch him and keep him in your room. He will bring you many prizes, which somebody did. I sprang to school sharing my newfound treasure. My excitement was squashed when my teacher did not believe me. She called Mom to tell her the tales I was voicing. Mama replied, "Do you not have leprechauns at your house?"

I don't think [that teacher] ever called her again.

In the summertime Mom would allow/require me to accompany crews on cleaning jobs. I assumed my position in a plastic box as a rag holder and rode up and down the lakeside roads to homes. It was an adventure to observe the trinkets of the rich. I got to see various works of art. I had never seen a hot tub or sauna baths either. Some had elevators and swimming pools.

Once she told me I could swim while they worked, neglecting to warn me there was a vacuum pool cleaner crawling around like a kid-eating monster. I ran back into the house and started dusting. How Mom could give me permission to be eaten alive in that dang pool??? She didn't have to tell me to do anything over that day.

The work was hard but a laugh was always near. Sometimes I hid behind shower curtains in bathrooms waiting for crew members to enter the room. They yanked the curtain open to find me standing with a Halloween mask on. It was a grand scene.

Can you imagine standing bedside with total focus on perfecting sheets and blankets only to hear violent growls and feel fingernails scratch your ankles? They always forgave me.

As I entered high school so did my appetite for sports. I started late because drives to practice were twenty miles away. My parents were tired at the end of the day and had little interest running the roads. I argued that attending school all day was more than working. They must have had scars in their tongues from not commenting on my idea.

I asked them to attend my soccer game, which they did, then left after admission fees were required. "We supplied the time, gasoline, and the kid to kick the dang ball, and YOU want us to pay?!" They did not stay to watch the game. I wasn't offended, in fact I felt a bit sorry for what the admission worker had to endure. The game went on and they went home.

I do plan to remain in the mountains because it's my home and they seem to filter some of the evil that overpowers other places. I don't know that anyone or anything can be done to persuade the residents to appreciate and protect their surroundings. Much of my appreciation is due to the fact that I grew up here. I have a strong connection to these hills as a result. I imagine that everyone has a similar allegiance with his or her birthplace. But as we know, many inhabitants of Rabun County came much later in life, so their allegiance may be different.

The changes that we have seen here within the past few years were said to be in the name of progress. Four lane highways, industry, and franchise food markets have replaced dirt roads, farming, and local food merchants. I can only think of two local merchants, Andy's Grocery and Reeves Hardware that would take a good man's word for future payment.

"REARED LIKE FRISKY COLTS"

I met Virginia Watts in 1997 as a co-worker at the Senior Center. I quickly discerned an eagle spirit inside that attracted others into her presence. Her wide wing span embraces everyone with a heart as soft as feathers yet strong enough to weather storms.

As native Appalachians we share a common faith and deep love for the mountains. She lives with Frank, her husband of 44 years, under the shadow of Big Face Mountain in Rabun County.

"The mountains give me a sense of protection from city distractions. I experience a moving awe in my soul here. A purer atmosphere and the wonderful people are the secret of the mountains. They contribute greatly to my life and security. I can depend on them to embrace me, understand me, lend helping hands, or just leave me alone to be who I am."

After she left the Senior Center, she began working as an assistant with young children in the local Head Start program at age fifty. With government assistance she began attending Gainesville State College and obtained a degree that enabled her to become a teacher in the Head Start classroom. She was a member of the Phi Theta Kappa National Honor Society. She overcomes disabling arthritis with the determination to make a difference in young lives.

Virginia Watts • Gainesville State College 2008

Virginia said, "The greatest challenge in teaching is to love the unlovable. I can only love each student by God's grace of unconditional love. If I don't love them, I cannot set a loving example as their instructor.

"Most of my students are from disadvantaged homes. If by definition, disadvantaged homes means poor, then I was disadvantaged; but we were taught manners and respect. Being disadvantaged is not an excuse for misbehavior as society now allows. In my classroom I must tolerate unthinkable actions by three and four year olds. Hitting, spitting, cursing and threatening teachers were unheard of when I was young. In my school days correction was swift and effective. State regulations restrict consequences to speaking with parents and notations of bad behavior in one of seven folders I must keep on each student. Head Start depends heavily on parent co-operation. I must applaud my Hispanic parents for their concern and support for their children.

"Working with children is like God working with me. Sometimes I don't always listen and follow instructions. Sometimes I get restless, tired, lazy or careless just like a child. But after the storms there is forgiveness and love."

Virginia introduced me to her elder brother Bob Justus. Bob has written for several local newspapers and penned over 500 poems pouring forth his heart and soul through an anointed pen dipped in rich mountain heritage. I have often joked to Virginia, "If I had a brother who could write like Bob, I'd make him set on the television with pen and paper for entertainment."

Bob said, "Virginia and I were most fortunate to be born to a loving farm family in our sheltered valley in the Appalachian Mountains and reared like frisky colts in Germany Valley under Big Face Mountain.

"Our Grandfather, Papa Jessie Justus, was a strong mentor. He lived between the sun and the soil, one of the first to practice land conservation. I carried a shovel behind him in the rain, opening standing puddles and building terraces to prevent erosion. Now, most are bulldozed down. He was a shepherd featured in *"The Foxfire Book."*

"Once, Papa Jessie came up to an isolated pasture to check on his sheep and bring salt. A roving dog had slain one and had its head buried in its vitals, eating away. It was on a cool, windy March day, and the wind hid Papa's approaching from the dog. With wild rage and a pocketknife, he grabbed that dog by the head and slit its throat. Another time, a wild night ensued as a pack of wild dogs got among the sheep. The noise was terrible. The next day at sunup, the men came from the community to find bloody clumps of sheep strewn in the pasture. They prowled the fields and woods for a week, killing stray dogs they did not recognize. There was never another raid on Papa's sheep."

Recently I asked Bob, "Have you seen the scars on your mountain lately?" His heart-touching and mind-pro- voking answer: "It's not my mountain anymore."

Bob Justus—Germany Valley.
Big Face Mountain in the background.

"BOB'S DREAM"

Bob is a proud veteran of two wars, Korea and Vietnam. He shared a powerful and reoccurring dream with me about change in the mountains he loves. Bob was in the military on strange soil, among strange people speaking strange tongues, when the dream occurred:

"At the head of the valley where brook trout finned, a rill came down from nearby Big Face Mountain. In a sunny glade fringed by tall trees, a sand bar lay by head-high ferns. As I rested from stalking trout, I dreamed of a host of angelic white butterflies swarming in a glade. They rested on the sand. I was in Korea when I dreamed this; years later, in Vietnam, the dream visited me again. When I finally got to come home, I visited the place I dreamed about. It had been sold to a Florida family. The tall, mighty oaks were gone. The beautiful ferns gave way to a man-made pond. A nice lawn covered the sand bar near the flashing stream. I wrote this poem:

There is a Place

There is a place where water flows
O'er polished gravel beds
Past ferns whose graceful heads
Bow to music no human knows
In this quiet glen where the thrush sings
I sit in silent awe
And hear notes without flaw
From an angel on feathered wings
Here butterflies as in a trance

Gather from near and far
To swarm o'er a sandbar
In weaving, dazzling dance
Great oaks stand in solemn parade
With boughs spread far and wide
Where birds and beasts may hide
And I can sit in cooling shade.
Each time I go to seek relief
And hear an angel sing
My spirit rises on quick wing
To soar above defeat or grief."

Virginia said, "I hope the mountains themselves remain without more houses poked into their bleeding sides. I hope the younger generation can roam trails soaked in inspiration as time marches on.

"Our ancestors once owned thousands of mountainous acres. Over the years the land was divided and sold to outsiders who put chains or gates across the property. Now, my generation owns very small parcels of ancestral land. Few mountain families have enough land to divide equally anymore among children and grandchildren. They have a greater challenge to go to college and earn land here if this is where they chose to stay. But, wherever younger generations put down roots, the God of the mountain lives within hearts all over the world. My hope is that they build on values we were taught and try to live by.

"I cherish memories. When I was no older than six, Mother allowed me to hold a small paring knife on lazy summer evenings as the entire family gathered around tubs of soft golden peaches that would become winter desserts. As ripened peach slices collected in kitchen bowls, rich conversation planted orchards inside our minds like the soft velvet on each peach.

"One day as we peeled peaches on the porch, it dawned on me that I had not seen our dog, Brownie. He, too, was ripe with age. My folks told me sometimes old dogs know when it is time to die; God gave them this knowledge. I was sad, blinking a few tears. They made Brownie's passing seem very dignified and dispelled the fear of death. I learned if God prepares his animals for change, how much greater am I."

CHANGE IS A GREAT CHALLENGE

In the early 1970s only about three major land developers operated in Rabun County. Forty years later, I have lost count of the land developers cutting and packaging mountain solace to the wealthy at a hefty price. Roadside billboards and ads advertize land as literal pieces of paradise.

Rapacious land developers did not invade the mountains like wild dogs among innocent sheep.

They came smiling with money in their hands. Mountain land is a money-generating giant. Homesteads were acquired for many reasons: aging landowners could no longer work the land for income; financial security was more important than acreage; medical bills or high taxes forced families to sell; some felt their children could better divide money than land; some did not have family to pass land to.

Old homesteads are laid bare by strange tracks from heavy earth moving equipment. Giant excavators chew and tear ton-sized bites from aged forest beds. Whitetail deer trails disappear. Sweet water springs vanish. Eagles are evicted from high places. Scenes of untamed beauty are replaced with towering elegantly-designed homes dotting ridges like spots on a leopard. They perch like spies above us through remaining forests. Bright security lights pollute the natural darkness and blot out the wonder of clear night skies. Cold reality stabs my heart like icicles in the voice of the freezing winds of change. It's not my mountain anymore.

The buyers come for the same reason our

The next three photos are "Scars of Progress"

ancestors did—seclusion and solace—and not all

(Note the old homestead at the bottom)

of them feel like intruders trampling over that which is sacred to us. Over the years I have come to learn and appreciate what transplants can offer, and realize that not all change has to be destructive.

RISING SAP

It's early March and the end of a cold hard winter. Red maple buds announce the rising of sap, the life-blood of the mountains. The forest awakens from winter slumber as a new cycle begins. In appointed times, seed by seed, bud by bud, branch by branch, person by person, are touched by the Master's will. All creation opens to declare the glory to the Creator. His glory is His goodness.

Wild dogwood blooming in the spring is a sight that can pierce the heart. Dad said there was a legend that dogwoods were once large trees until a Cross was hewn from their timbers. Afterwards its growth was twisted and spindly. The blooms themselves tell the old, old story. Four white petals, pierced and stained red, form a cross that has at its center a crown of thorns. Out of respect, Dad forbid the burning of dogwood trees.

Wise Solomon said, "A good man leaveth an inheritance to his children's children." Dad was a good man, protecting our birthright long after he passed on. Family land sales must first be offered to existing heirs at a fair and reasonable price. Dad instilled the value of inheritance deep within his children. "Don't ever mortgage your hat; you need a roof. Corn won't grow and eagles can't fly inside a land developer's safe deposit box. What will you do for money when all the land is gone? You will have no place to come back to, no place to call home. The love of money will take your freedom, and you will be cornered by the rich whose garage is worth more than your house."

The greatest inheritance my family gave me is Christ. HE literally walked this earth within their hearts.

Mountain climbing, wherever it may be, is a personal journey to the top. The same life-giving rays of the sun that shone down on early pioneers long ago shine on each generation with equal illumination and opportunity to make a difference in our world. Those men and women were not immune to change, but found a way to cope as we must also—that is what makes pioneers.

My hope for future generations is they determine that the mountain's destiny will be in their

hands, and not deliver what remains to commercial rapists who sell high priced lots far beyond native's reach. May they become involved and committed in preservation.

I hope they build themselves on faith-filled tomorrows skipping through fields and trails, among groves of wildflowers with their pockets full of sunshine and occasionally remember their heritage. I hope they find a sweet water spring to cool their lips as they drink deep the blessings of God's pastures.

CREDITS

CHAPTER 3

1.Noah Webster, *"The Elementary Spelling Book"* (New York: Americian Book Company, 1857)

CHAPTER 7

1.Eliot Wigginton, *"Sometimes a Shining Moment"* (New York: Doubleday,1995)
Ibid.,p.9
1.Eliot Wigginton, *"The Foxfire Book"* (New York: Doubleday, 1972) Ibid.,p.9-10

1.Eliot Wigginton, *"Moments"* (Star Press,1975) Ibid.,p.23
2.Eliot Wigginton, *"Foxfire 2"* (New York: Random House, 1973) Ibid.,p.25-27

CHAPTER 10

1.Vulcan Material Company (Customer Invoice)

CHAPTER 11

1.Foxfire Magazine, 1973 Winter Issue (Introduction, Centerfold p.300-312)
2.Eliot Wigginton, *"Sometimes A Shining Moment"* (New York:Doubleday,1995)
3.Rabun County Official Ordinance And Subdivision Regulations 2003

For additional copies of this book, please complete
on a separate sheet of paper the following details:

Name _____

Address _____

_____

Phone (in case of returns) _____

_____ books @ $20.00 = _____

Tax @ GA 7%= _____

Shipping and Handling
$3.50 per book   _____

Total of order   _____

Send to the following address:

It's Not My Mountain Anymore
P.O. Box 93
Rabun Gap, GA 30568

❏ I am interested in receiving more information
about how to acquire Barbara Taylor Woodall as a
speaker for our club or civic meeting, dinner
meeting,book club, a book signing...or

_____.

Check out the website:
www.itsnotmymountainanymore.com